WAY TO PLAY
SOCCER

THIS IS A CARLTON BOOK

This edition published by Carlton Books 1995

ISBN 1-85868-155-3

Printed and bound in Spain

Illustrations by Oliver Frey

PHOTOGRAPHIC ACKNOWLEDGMENTS
The publishers would like to thank the following sources for their kind permission to reproduce the pictures used in this publication:
Allsport; Colorsport and Bob Thomas Sports Photography.

THE AUTHOR
PETER STEWART was the editor of *Shoot* – Britain's best-selling soccer magazine – for eight years. He then became managing editor of the football group at IPC Magazines Ltd., which included *Shoot*, *World Soccer*, *Soccerstars* and *90 Minutes*, all top selling soccer titles. He is now freelance editorial consultant to the football group and also edits the West Ham United FC Matchday programme and has compiled several reference books. He is an enthusiastic supporter of the world-famous Coerver Coaching programme and has promoted the development of this coaching system in the UK. He is also the UK representative for the Dallas International Youth Tournament and a founder member of the Association of Soccer Coaches and Teachers, and works closely with soccer personalities such as Trevor Brooking, Don Howe, Ray Clemence and Gordon Strachan.

WAY TO PLAY

SOCCER

THE FULL-COLOUR GUIDE TO MAXIMIZING YOUR SKILLS

Peter Stewart

CARLTON

Contents

Introduction

SOCCER is one of the easiest games to play. It is also the most popular and exciting contact sport in the world with over 117 million players—among them six million women—spread throughout 175 countries. It is watched by billions of fans in stadia and on television throughout the world. The 1994 World Cup, the first finals to be staged in the USA, attracted a world-wide TV audience of 31.5 billion.

"The Beautiful Game", as soccer was once described by Pele, perhaps the greatest player of all-time, is also "The People's Game". It can be played anywhere and on almost any kind of surface. The great Pele is just one of hundreds of top stars who learned their skills kicking a tennis ball, or tin can, along a beach or back-street in some remote town or village around the world. The game gives players the opportunity to combine individual skills with the strength and discipline of teamwork... and spectators the thrill and passion of watching players and teams display the different tactics and variety of techniques that makes it so special.

This book, Way-To-Play Soccer, is aimed at providing players of all ages and skill with a better understanding of the game. Even today's great players (such as Ryan Giggs, Alan Shearer, Roberto Baggio, Dennis Bergkamp, Jürgen Klinsmann and Romario) need to practise and work hard at perfecting their skills. They also need good knowledge of the Laws of the Game to play the game in the right spirit, promote fair play and prove a worthy inspiration to young players hoping to follow in their bootsteps.

The first section of this book explains in detail the 17 Laws of the Game, including the least understood and most controversial of them all, the offside rule. The second section provides hundreds of tips that are of enormous benefit to all young players. All the game's skills, tactics and techniques are brought to life with specially commissioned full-colour illustrations and diagrams, and there are tips on passing, shooting, heading, trapping, dribbling, tackling, plus a special chapter devoted to goalkeeping. The book also includes an analysis of advanced techniques for experienced players, such as the glancing header, the overhead kick and the swerved pass with the outside of the foot.

The third section comprises of a study of soccer tactics, including modern-game team formations, attacking and defensive strategies, and set-piece plays, such as corner-kicks, free-kicks and throw-ins. The book is packed with Way-To-Play tips and photographs of today's top players in action. Finally, there's a two-page glossary of key soccer terms and an index.

Reading this book and using it to practise the skills and techniques explained in its pages will help you get more satisfaction out of the game and become a better player—whatever skill level you are aiming to achieve.

PETER STEWART

The Rules of the Game

TO play and enjoy soccer you should be fit and have a good sense of balance, be prepared to practise to improve your skills, and understand the rules. Without a thorough knowledge of the 17 Laws of the Game neither players nor spectators will never really appreciate or be allowed to develop the finer points of the game.

 1 THE FIELD OF PLAY

Dimensions

The soccer pitch is rectangular to ensure the flow of play between the two goals. Its length must not be more than 130 yards (120m) nor less than 100 yards (90m). The width must not be more than 100 yards (90m) or less than 50 yards (45m). The pitch cannot be square

The Goal Area

This is generally known as the 'six-yard box' and is formed by measuring six yards (5.5m) from the inside of each goal post along the goal line. Two lines then extend six yards into the Field Of Play at right-angles to the goal line. These lines are then connected by a line running parallel to the goal line. The main purpose of the Goal Area is to indicate where goal kicks should be taken.

The Goals

These are the most important pieces of equipment on the Field Of Play. They are placed on the centre of each goal line and consist of two upright posts, eight yards (7.32m) apart, joined by a horizontal crossbar which must be eight feet (2.44m) from the ground. The width and depth of the goalposts and crossbar must not exceed five inches (12cm). They must be made of wood, metal or other approved material and are white so they can easily be seen. Nets are attached to the posts and crossbars. They should be properly pegged down at the sides and behind the goal to ensure they don't sag and impede the goalkeeper, or allow the ball to pass underneath.

The Penalty Area

At each end of the pitch, two lines are drawn at right-angles to the goal line, 18 yards (16.5m) from each goal post. These extend 18 yards into the Field Of Play and are joined by a line drawn parallel to the goal line. This defines the area in which the goalkeeper can handle the ball. A mark is then made within each penalty area 12 yards (11m) from the mid-point of each goal line. This is called the penalty spot. From this spot an arc of a circle with a radius of ten yards (9.1m) is drawn outside the penalty area. This arc indicates the minimum distance players must be from the ball when a penalty kick is being taken.

Way-To-Play Tips

Check lines

When you arrive at the ground, always check the pitch to ensure that all lines are clearly marked. Occasionally, lines may be unclear due to bad weather or because the groundsman hasn't re-marked the pitch after the last game. Also check that the lines are not rutted because ruts can cause injury to players who catch their ankles in them.

The Corner Area

A small quarter-circle with a one yard (1m) radius is drawn from each corner flagpost inside the Field Of Play. This shows the area where the ball must be placed when a corner kick is taken.

Marking

The Field Of Play is marked with clear and distinctive (usually white) lines, not more than five inches (12cm) in width. The longer boundary lines are called touchlines and the shorter lines are the goal lines. Flag posts at least five feet (1.5m) high are placed at each corner of the pitch. Similar flag posts may be placed at the halfway line, not less than one yard (1m) outside the touchline, although these are optional.

The Field Of Play is divided into two halves by a halfway line. The centre of the pitch is indicated with a suitable mark for the kick-off and a circle with a ten-yard (9.1m) radius is marked around it. This is known as the centre circle and enables the referee to ensure the opposing team is standing at least ten yards from the ball at the kick-off.

② THE BALL

The ball must be spherical and made of leather or other approved materials, with a circumference of between 27–28 inches (67.5–70cm) and a weight of 14–16 oz (396–453g). The referee should inspect it before a match to ensure it is neither too hard nor too soft. It should not be changed during a game unless authorised by the referee. Spare balls should always be available.

③ NUMBER OF PLAYERS

A match is played by two teams, each consisting of 11 players, one of whom must be the goalkeeper. In addition, substitutes, usually three, can be used depending on the rules of the competition. Substitutes can only enter the Field Of Play during a stoppage in the game and after they have received a signal from the referee. The substitute must enter the Field Of Play at the halfway line, and only after the player being replaced has left the pitch. Once substituted, a player cannot return to the game. If a substitute has been sent off after play has started, he cannot be replaced. In certain competitions, such as the FA Premiership, a goalkeeper is among the named substitutes. But any player can change places with the goalkeeper, provided the referee's permission is obtained and the player wears the appropriate jersey.

upper foot
outside foot
outstep
heel
toe
inside foot
instep

Boots may have studs or bars for grip that conform to rigid standards to protect other players. This is a left boot pictured above and below.

④ PLAYERS' EQUIPMENT

The football strip, or kit, consists of a shirt (or jersey for goalkeepers), shorts, socks, shinguards and football boots. Two types of boot are used – the moulded-sole for hard, dry pitches and the screw-in studded boot for softer surfaces. The function of studs, usually made of plastic, rubber, aluminium or other suitable material, is to prevent players from slipping. The advantage to screw-in studs is that they can be changed to suit the conditions – longer studs providing better grip on wet and muddy surfaces, and shorter ones more suitable for dry grounds.

Each player on a team must wear the same coloured shirts and, to avoid confusion, this colour must be different from the opposition's shirts. Goalkeepers must wear distinctively coloured jerseys to distinguish them from the outfield players and referee. The goalkeeper may also wear gloves to improve his grip on the ball and a cap to keep the sun from his eyes. Numbers are usually displayed on the back of a player's shirt or goalkeeper's jersey.

Players should always take a pride in their appearance.

Shin guards must be worn to protect a player's shin.

Way-To-Play Tips

Ball work

Always carry a spare ball, pump and valve adaptors, you'd be surprised how many clubs don't. The referee must check that the match and spare balls are correctly inflated. If a ball is too hard it will bounce excessively, too soft and the ball will be 'lifeless' with little bounce, making it difficult to pass accurately.

Keep boots clean

The most important part of the kit is your boots, so make sure they are comfortable. Boots that are too small can damage your feet, and if they are too big it can be hard to get a good feel of the ball.

5 REFEREES

A referee is appointed to control the game. The referee's authority and the powers granted under the Laws of the Game take effect immediately on entering the Field Of Play. The referee enforces the Laws of the Game; keeps a record of the game; acts as timekeeper and can add on time lost through treatment of injuries or other causes; stops the game at injuries and infringements; can caution or send-off offending players; may suspend or end the game before normal time because of bad weather, trouble caused by spectators, or any other incident that makes such action necessary. The referee's decision on the Field Of Play is final and should not be disputed. The referee should wear colours distinctive from the shirts worn by the two opposing teams. No person other than the players and linesmen may enter the Field Of Play without the referee's permission. A referee should take the following items on to the Field Of Play: pencil, notebook, whistle, coin, spare whistle, stopwatch, wristwatch, spare pencil, yellow and red cards.

Referees have to pass an exam which tests their knowledge of the Laws of the Game, and courses are held regularly. Players are encouraged to go on a referee's course so that they get a better understanding of football. It is amazing, but many top players do not know all the Laws of the Game.

George Courtney was England's top referee in the late 1980s/early 1990s and officiated in the 1990 World Cup.

6 LINESMEN

Two linesmen are appointed for each match. Their function is to assist the referee in accordance with the Laws. The linesmen, one on each touchline, indicate to the referee when the ball is out of play and signal corner kicks, goal kicks or throw-ins.

If an infringement by a player on either team is spotted, the linesman raises a vividly coloured flag to attract the referee's attention, who can then decide whether to act on this signal or not. One of the linesman's most important tasks is to signal to the referee when an attacking player strays offside.

Linesmen flag signals: throw-in (above) and substitution (right).

The linesman indicates (clockwise from the top) offside: when play has stopped; the position on the far side of the field; centre of the field; and near side of the field.

7 GAME DURATION

The game is played over two equal periods of 45 minutes (known as halves), unless otherwise agreed upon by the two teams. Any time lost through injury, time-wasting or substitutions can be added on at the referee's discretion. Extra time is also allowed for a player to take a penalty kick if one is awarded at, or after, the end of normal time in either half. The half-time interval should not exceed 15 minutes except by consent of the referee. However, it is common to have half-time intervals of more extended periods at some televised matches.

8 THE START OF PLAY

To start a game, the two captains toss a coin for choice of ends, or the right to kick-off. Before the kick-off, the referee should ensure the ball is stationary on the centre spot.

Opponents must not come into the centre circle – within ten yards (9.1m) of the ball – until the ball has been kicked. On the referee's whistle, the game is started by a player kicking the ball forwards.

Once played, the ball must travel its own circumference before being touched by another player. The player kicking-off must not play the ball again until it has been touched by another player. The game should be restarted in the same manner, although at the start of the second half the teams should change ends. The team which didn't kick-off in the first half has the second-half kick-off.

9 BALL IN AND OUT OF PLAY

The ball is out of play when (a) the whole of the ball has crossed the goal or touchlines, either on the ground or in the air and (b) when the game has been stopped by the referee. The ball is in play at all other times, including when it rebounds off the goalposts, crossbar, corner flags or the referee.

OUT OF PLAY

FIELD OF PLAY

Whether in the air or on the ground, the ball is only deemed to be out of play when the whole of its circumference has crossed the goal line or touchlines. In this illustration, only the balls on the red lines are out of play.

In this illustration, only the ball in the pale blue area at the top counts as having crossed the goal line. If the goalkeeper were to stop any of the others at their current positions, the goal will have been saved.

10 SCORING

A goal is scored when the whole of the ball crosses the goal line, either on the ground or in the air, between the goalposts and under the cross-bar. The team scoring the most goals wins the game. If the number of goals scored is equal the result is a draw.

THE Offside Law is the most misunderstood and controversial of all the rules. Many players, even top internationals, are often unaware exactly when they are offside. The first thing to remember is that your position when you receive the ball is irrelevant. What matters is your position when the ball is actually played forwards.

If, at the moment the ball is passed, there are less than two defenders between an attacker and the goal, the attacker is offside – remember the goalkeeper usually counts as one of the two defenders. When you are attacking if you are level with the last defender with only the goalkeeper in front of you, you are not offside.

Exceptions

There are three occasions when positioning is not relevant, even when the ball is played. They are:

(1) from a goal kick; or

(2) from a throw-in; or

(3) from a corner kick.

But in each case as soon as the ball is touched by a team-mate, a player can be offside. Players can also be offside from a free kick, a drop-kick or throw from the goalkeeper.

An attacking player can also be offside if the ball bounces off a team-mate and goes forwards to the attacker, even if an opposing defender is the last player to deliberately kick or head the ball. If a team-mate's forward pass touches a defender and goes to an attacker in an offside position with no defenders closer to the goal line, the player is still offside.

Other times when an attacker is not offside with no defenders closer to the goal line, are when the ball is passed backwards by a team-mate who is closer to goal (however, when the receiving player shoots, the team-mate may be offside), or if a player is in his own half of the field when the ball is played. The new rule brought in for the 1994 World Cup

Finals states that a player shall not be declared offside unless, when in an offside position, he makes an active attempt to play the ball. This means a player can now stand anywhere on the field as long as he is not in line with the goalkeeper without being offside. Only when a team-mate passes the ball to him, or he deliberately runs towards the ball will he declared offside.

BELOW AND OPPOSITE: three examples of onside and offside positions. Yellow lines represent the path of the ball, red lines the movement of players. Attackers are in red, defenders in blue shirts and yellow shorts. The goalkeeper is in grey.

Player (A) is OFFSIDE because there is only one defender (the goalkeeper) between him and the goal when the ball is played.

Interfering with play

At this point, it is worth thinking about the phrase, 'not interfering with play'. Usually, this only happens when the ball is crossed backwards from the wings. At a corner, for instance, the corner taker may be the closer to the goal line than any defender, but is clearly not interfering with play.

Player (A) is OFFSIDE because although defender (X) is closer to the goal, goalkeeper (Y) defender (Z) are actually in front of (A), so there is only one defender between the attacker and the goal.

Player (A) is ONSIDE. Although only the goalkeeper is closer to the goal line than the front two attackers, because Player (B) has run past two defenders (from B1–B2), the eventual cross has been pulled back to Player (A).

If you realise that you are in an offside position as an attack develops, you may be tempted to step off the field to indicate non-interference with play. But this will result in a caution from the referee for leaving the field without permission.

If you get injured, the referee or linesman may consider you to be 'not interfering with play', but if you then get up and run after the ball, you may be declared offside.

Free kick

The referee will award an indirect free kick to the opposing team if a player is declared offside. This is taken from the spot where the infringement occurred, unless the offence is committed by a player in the opponents' goal area. In this case, the free kick should be taken from any point within the goal area.

Offside Trap

This tactic is often used by defenders to force attackers deliberately offside. While marking the attackers as they wait for a pass, the defenders suddenly move out in a line as the ball is about to be played, leaving the attackers stranded in an offside position, or forcing them to play the ball back towards their own goal.

Using this tactic successfully requires good teamwork and discipline. Used properly, it is an effective method of frustrating attacks. But defenders should not get complacent since the trap can be beaten by an attacker dribbling the ball through the defensive line, or a quick passing movement.

Way-To-Play Tips

Be aware

If you are your team's most forward attacker it is your responsibility to ensure you stay onside by (a) remaining behind the ball; (b) keeping at least two opponents between you and the goal line; and (c) keeping well clear of the action if you find yourself in an offside position.

Timing

Practise making timed runs to beat the defenders' offside trap. If you time your run perfectly and the pass is a good one, you will have a free run at goal.

Accept the decision

In the vast majority of cases linesmen make the right decisions. Anything said to a linesman after his ruling will be ignored (or punished with a caution), so accept his decision – even if you are certain it is not the right one – and get on the with game.

An attacker scores while a team-mate is standing in an offside position. But because he is not interfering with play, he should not be penalised for offside and the goal will stand.

12 FOULS AND MISCONDUCT

LAW 12 was not devised to discourage the physical effort needed to play the game. It provides a code of discipline to enable you to display your skills in a physical contact game by protecting you against unnecessary force and foul play. Law 12 comprises three parts: (a) Major Offences, (b) Other Offences and (c) Misconduct.

The Major Offences

There are nine major, or penal offences which, if committed intentionally, are penalised by awarding a direct free kick to the opposing team. Eight of the nine offences are concerned with physical foul play against opponents. Should a defending player intentionally commit any of these nine offences within the penalty area, a penalty kick will be awarded.

The penal offences are:

(1) Kicking, or attempting to kick an opponent;

(2) Tripping an opponent using the legs or stooping in front of, or behind, an opponent;

(3) Jumping at an opponent;

(4) Charging in a violent or dangerous manner;

(5) Charging an opponent from behind in a violent or dangerous manner (unless the opponent is guilty of obstruction);

(6) Striking, attempting to strike, or spitting at an opponent;

(7) Holding an opponent with the hand or arm;

(8) Pushing an opponent;

(9) Handling the ball with any part of the hand or arm.

Other Non-penal Offences

Offences penalised with an indirect free kick are:

(1) Dangerous play (attempting to kick the ball while held by the goalkeeper, attempting to kick a ball close to the head of an opponent);

(2) Charging an opponent fairly, but while not attempting to play the

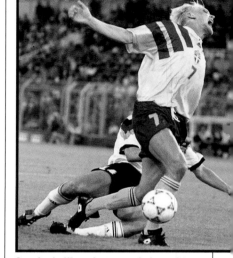

Sweden's Klaus Ingesson is brought down from behind.

ball (shoulder charging an opponent fairly, but when the ball is not within playing distance);

(3) Obstruction (blocking an opponent's path to the ball when it is not within playing distance);

(4) Charging the goalkeeper (unless he is holding the ball, obstructing an opponent, or has gone outside his goal area);

(5) Goalkeeper not releasing the ball into play properly (when more than four steps are taken while holding, bouncing or throwing the ball in the air before releasing it. After releasing the ball, the goalkeeper is not allowed to touch it again with his hands until it has been played by

Whether intentional or not, tripping up an opponent is foul play. Here the culprit is clearly not aiming for the ball in the tackle.

another player. He is, however, permitted to play the ball with his feet);

(6) Time-wasting by the goalkeeper (if the referee considers the ball is held for an unreasonable time, or the goalkeeper indulges in other tactics considered by the referee to be wasting time to unfairly give advantage to his own team);

(7) If a team-mate deliberately passes with the foot to the goalkeeper and the keeper uses his hand or hands to control the ball. A good referee will let the keeper know if he can handle a sliced clearance, or tackle.

The 'Professional Foul'

If you are denied an obvious goal-scoring opportunity by an opponent deliberately handling the ball, or by unfairly impeding your path to goal, it is classed as serious foul play and the referee should dismiss the offender from the Field Of Play.

Misconduct

To avoid committing offences, all players should understand the Laws of the Game, accept the referee's decisions without argument, and conduct themselves as sportsmen. Referees will caution you by showing the yellow card, and award an indirect free kick to the opposing team, if you:

(1) enter, or reenter the Field Of Play after the game has started, or leave the Field of Play during the game (except through accident), without first gaining permission from the referee;

(2) show by word or action, dissent from any refereeing decision;

(3) are guilty of ungentlemanly conduct;

(4) persistently infringe the Laws of the Game.

The referee will show you the red card and send you off if you are guilty of:

A player will be shown the red card, and sent off, for serious foul play.

(1) violent conduct, or serious foul play;

(2) use foul and abusive language;

(3) are guilty of a second yellow card offence after previously receiving a caution.

If the referee stops play to dismiss a player without that player having committed a foul (for example, the player might have sworn at the linesman or left the field without permission) the game will resume with an indirect free kick to the opposing team from the place where the infringement took place.

Dangerous play, such as kicking at a high ball in another player's face, is an offence which will be penalised.

Way-To-Play Tips

Ungentlemanly conduct

Often a player will shout 'My ball!' or 'Leave it!' when going for the ball. Opponents can be distracted by this and hesitate when making a challenge for the ball. If you do shout always use a player's name, for example: 'Bill King's ball!' or 'Goalkeeper's ball!' Holding an opponent back by his shirt, or climbing on his back to gain extra height are two other examples of unfair play.

Above all, remember a referee's decision is final – don't argue with referee or linesmen, or you could get booked for dissent.

13 FREE KICKS

A free kick can be either direct or indirect and is always taken from the spot where the offence occurred (except for a penalty kick, below). The ball must be stationary when the kick is taken and it must be touched by another player before the kicker is allowed to strike it again. While a player can score from a direct free kick, a goal cannot be scored from an indirect free kick until the ball has been touched by another player. To indicate that a free-kick is indirect the referee will raises one arm above his head.

When defending a free kick, players must be at least ten yards (9.1m) from the ball, except when an

The referee clearly indicates why he has awarded a free kick against an offending player.

indirect free kick has been awarded less than ten yards from the goal. Opponents may then stand between the goalposts or on the goalline.

If the defending team is awarded a free kick in its own penalty area, the ball must be kicked out of the area and no opponents may enter the area until the kick is taken.

Manchester United's Dennis Irwin takes the perfect penalty kick.

14 THE PENALTY KICK

A penalty kick often proves crucial in a match, indeed a penalty proved to be a World Cup winner for Germany in the 1990 final when Brehme converted his spotkick in the 85th minute to give his side victory against Argentina.

A penalty – a free shot on goal taken from the penalty spot – is awarded if the defending team commits a foul inside its own penalty area that would normally be punished by a direct free kick. All players, with the exception of the goalkeeper and the player taking the kick, must stand outside the penalty area, at least ten yards (9.15m) from the penalty spot.

There are a three basic rules regarding penalty kicks:

(1) the goalkeeper must stand on the goal-line until the ball is kicked (his feet must not move but he may sway his body);

(2) the player taking the kick must kick the ball forwards;

(3) the penalty-taker must not touch the ball a second time until it has been touched by another player.

As penalty kicks are a vital part of the game, time can be extended at half time or full time to allow them to be taken, or retaken. There are only three reasons why a kick should be retaken, these are if:

(1) the defending team breaks the Law and a goal is not scored;

(2) the attacking team, with the exception of the kicker, infringes and a goal is scored;

(3) there are infringements by players of both teams. If the kicker breaks the Law (by playing the ball twice for example) the defending team is awarded an indirect free kick.

⑮ THROW-IN

Originally designed as a means of getting the ball back into play as quickly as possible, the throw-in has developed into an effective attacking technique. Some players, such as England's Stuart Pearce, have developed a 'long throw', that is almost as effective as a corner if it is awarded close to the opponent's penalty-area.

The throw-in should be taken along the touchline at the point where the ball went out of play, and the ball must be thrown into play with both hands, from behind and over the head. The thrower must face the Field Of Play and, as the ball is released, part of each foot must be on the ground on, or behind, the touchline.

If these rules are broken, or the thrower attempts to gain an unfair advantage by moving along the touchline, the throw-in will be given to the opposing team.

A goal cannot be scored direct from a throw-in, and the thrower may not touch the ball again until it has been touched by another player.

For the throw-in, the throwing player must have both feet on or behind the touchline, and at least a part of both feet must remain in contact with the ground during the throw. Both hands, placed either side of the ball (or behind it in the case of a long throw, see pages 42–43), must be used for the throw-in.

⑯ GOAL KICK

Goal kicks (kicks taken from within the goal area returning the ball into play) are awarded to the defending team when the ball crosses its goal line, outside the goal, after having last been touched by an opponent.

Although goalkeepers generally take goal kicks, they may be taken by any other player. When taking a goal kick the ball must travel outside the penalty area, although a 'short goal kick' (a pass to a defender standing just outside the penalty-area) is a good way of retaining possession and setting-up an attack.

A long goal kick – especially if there is a strong tail wind – can be very effective, because forwards cannot be offside from a goal kick. A goal cannot be scored direct from a goal kick, and if this happens the game is restarted with a goal kick to the opposing team. It is a corner if the ball blows into the kicker's net.

The corner kick must be taken from within the quarter-circle, so the ball at position B will not be allowed.

⑰ CORNER KICK

A corner kick is awarded to the attacking team if the ball crosses the goal line, either in the air on the ground, having last been played by one of the defending team. It is taken from the quarter-circle by the corner flag on the appropriate side of the pitch. The flag must not be removed to take the kick, and opponents must stand at least ten yards (9.1m) away from the ball until it is in play. As with a free kick, the kicker must not play the ball again until it has been touched by another player, although unlike an indirect free kick, a goal can be scored direct from a corner kick.

Skills and Techniques

TO be a soccer success, you need a combination of natural skill and dedication to constantly improve your techniques. You need to master the basic skills of the game, and must be able to control the ball, pass it to a team-mate, shoot with either foot, head the ball and tackle opponents when necessary – in fact, develop a good balance of skills relating to the position you play. You will also need the vision to read games and playing situations. One thing's for sure, no matter if you are an international star, or whether you play for fun, you can never learn enough about the game.

① KICKING THE BALL

BEING able to kick the ball correctly is the most important basic skill in the game to master. You need total control of the ball to ensure it goes where you want it to at the right pace.

Any part of the foot can be used to kick the ball, although you should avoid kicking with your toes, because control is more difficult with this part of the foot.

Most players can kick a stationary ball quite easily, but you need to concentrate and to practise all the different kicking techniques to be able to take corner kicks, free kicks and to pass, cross and shoot properly during match-play action.

Holland's Dennis Bergkamp (7) shoots for goal against Denmark.

The pass with inside of the foot

The inside of your foot is the area from your heel to big toe. This kicking area is used for short, accurate low passes of up to 20 yards (18m). This is the easiest way of passing the ball to a team-mate because such a large area of foot is used for the kick.

To make the pass, place the non-kicking foot alongside the ball and point it in the direction you wish to send the ball, keeping your head down and eyes over it as you prepare to kick. Now, raise your kicking foot two to three inches (5–8cm) off the ground, turning it out almost at right-angles. Keeping the ankle firm, bring your foot back and strike the ball firmly in its centre. Finally, follow through with your kicking foot to guide the ball in the intended direction.

England's Chris Waddle and Romania's World Cup star Gheorghe Hagi are superb pass-masters of the ball over short, or long distances. You may recall Hagi's defence-splitting pass two minutes from the end of Romania's 1994 World Cup finals quarter-final tie against Sweden.

The score was 1–0 to Sweden when Hagi's pass into the penalty box was met by Florin Raducioiu, who made no mistake from close range. That took the game into extra-time, after which Sweden won 5–4 on penalties.

The pass with the outside of the foot

The outside of the foot is the flat area from the ankle to the end of the toes. It's difficult to kick the ball straight using this area, so it is used – mainly by experienced players – to curl, or bend the ball in flight. The knee and kicking foot are turned inwards and the outside front of the foot makes contact with the ball. Raise the kicking foot off the ground slightly and strike the centre of the ball. This skill is useful when faced with an opponent moving in to challenge you – flick the ball away to one side to a team-mate, or bend it around the challenger.

To ensure a powerful and accurate lofted kick use the instep of the foot, strike beneath the ball and use a full follow-through.

Kicking the ball with the outside of the foot is perfect for swerving passes or shots.

The lofted kick

The instep of the foot is used for long distance passes over the heads of opponents, crossing the ball into the area or corner kicks. To make the kick, lean backwards with the supporting foot to the side of and slightly behind the ball. Once in position, strike beneath the ball to give you the necessary lift and follow through with a full leg swing.

Soccer Practice

A good way to Improve your accuracy is to kick a ball against a wall that has been marked with numbered targets. Start by aiming for target box 1. If you hit it, go for box 2 and so on. You can practise this on your own or with several players. When you miss the target, it is another player's turn. Every time it's your turn, aim for the target you missed last time. As your accuracy improves, move further and further away from the target and shoot from different angles.

Set up two cones (or similar objects) a small distance apart. Aim to kick the ball between the cones to a friend, who kicks the ball back.

Split your team into two lines on either side of a goal. Have one player from each group throw the ball at varying angles for each player in turn to trap and then kick towards goal.

Stand between two players who are about 30 yards (27m) apart. As they lob the ball over your head, attempt to head it away. If you're successful, change places with one of the kickers. As your heading ability improves, try using two footballs.

In a marked area, players at each end bend the ball around a defender who is positioned in the middle.

The chip shot

If performed correctly, this is one of the most dangerously rewarding attacking kicks in the game. The chip shot can be used to score goals by lifting the ball over the goalkeeper's head if he has strayed too far off his line, open up the tightest of defences to put a team-mate in a good attacking position and to clear your lines if under pressure. To play a chip shot place the kicking foot and instep under the ball and flick your ankle. To make the ball rise steeply, there should a short leg backlift and very little follow-through.

The volley: note how the player swivels on the non-kicking foot and uses the instep of the other foot to strike the ball. Fine judgment of the ball's flight and pace is essential. The kick is made before the ball hits the ground.

The half-volley requires the same concentration and judgment as the volley, but the ball is struck after hitting the ground. Again, the instep should be the striking area to ensure power and to control the low trajectory.

With a stabbing movement, strike the ball on its underside for the chip shot. A ball rolling towards you is easier to chip accurately than a stationary one.

The volley and half-volley

One of soccer's most spectacular sights is a goal scored from a long-range volley. France's controversial superstar Eric Cantona practises volleying the ball every day during training, and has delighted fans with many stunning goals scored this way. Timing and concentration are vital for accuracy, and for maximum power the instep should be used to strike the ball.

Keep your eyes firmly on the ball when preparing for a volley, and try to judge the ball's line of flight and pace. Leaning back away from the ball, balance on the non-kicking foot, swivel your body and strike the ball before it hits the ground – pointing the toes downwards helps give extra power. Once contact is made, follow through with the kicking leg.

The half-volley is when you kick the ball just after it has hit the ground. Like the volley, the half-volley requires full concentration and good judgment to predict the ball's flight.

To kick a ball on the half-volley, place your non-kicking foot close to the spot where you estimate the ball is going to bounce. As it hits the ground, swing your kicking foot to make contact with the bouncing ball using the instep. Be sure to follow through the ball, keeping the kicking foot pointing down and forwards to give the ball a low trajectory and maximise the shot's power.

Unorthodox kicks

Overhead kicks, also known as bicycle kicks, can be used to catch goalkeepers by surprise, or to get a player out of trouble in defence. If the kick comes off and a spectacular goal is scored, you are a hero. If it doesn't you can be left flat on your back, out of the action and looking like a clown.

As the ball comes over, your kicking foot should be at full stretch, with your toes reaching for it. Impact with the ball should be made with the flat of the foot on the bootlace area, with the toes pointed towards your instep. Bend the knee of the non-kicking leg to ensure your body leans backwards. Bend your elbows and spread your hands to break your fall. Welsh international striker Mark Hughes is an expert at the overhead kick, or volley.

A swerving or curved pass can be used to make an inswinging corner-kick, or to swerve the ball around a defensive wall. The inside or outside of the foot may be used to curve the ball. Striking the ball's left side curves it to the right, and striking its right side curves it to the left. Leaning your body over the ball helps you gain greater control.

Way-To-Play Tips

Two feet
Always practise kicking the ball using both feet. Most players favour either the left or the right foot, but you need to concentrate more on your weaker foot.

Balance and power
The non-kicking foot is vital for accuracy and power. It should be positioned next to the ball when it is kicked – not in front of or behind it. Make sure it points in the direction you want the ball to travel, and to ensure a good contact keep your eyes firmly on the ball at all times.

The bicycle kick is certainly the most visually exciting of the unorthodox kicks, requiring almost a somersault. Make sure that your elbows are bent and hands outstretched to break your fall.

INSET: the back-heel kick can be used to deceive opponents. Step over the ball you are dribbling, stop suddenly and use the heel to kick the ball back to a team-mate in position.

The back-heel

This technique can be used effectively to wrong-foot opponents. For example, you can deceive a opponent by shaping to dribble the ball past the challenger then suddenly stopping, stepping over the ball and back-heeling it to a team-mate, leaving your opponent stranded. A word of caution, though, never attempt a back heel in front of your own goal.

When performing a back-heel, the supporting leg should be close to the ball. For power and accuracy, always try to strike the middle of the ball with the back of the heel. A slower, but more accurate method of back-heeling is to use the sole of the boot to stop the ball before making contact. Only use this method if you have plenty of time.

THE aim of all soccer matches is to score more goals than your opponents. Quality goalscorers are essential to every team, that's why strikers with a proven goal-scoring record, like English star Andy Cole, are among soccer's most wanted men and are worth a fortune in today's transfer market. Cole joined Manchester United from Newcastle United in January 1995 for a new British record fee of £7 million.

Although the goalscorer usually gets all the praise, the build-up to a goal requires team-work, keeping possession of the ball, building an attack and opening defences to create space in front of goal for the strikers to finish.

Many strikers are natural, goal-hungry predators who rely on pure instinct – nothing is more important to them then seeing the back of the net bulge.

Confidence, pace, height, control and body strength are a striker's vital assets. A striker also needs to be brave to stand the knocks that occur in the penalty area. England striker Alan Shearer and Germany's Jürgen Klinsmann are classic examples of the all-round, all-action striker. They have the ability to use all their skills and power while under pressure.

As a goalscorer you need a sixth sense of where the goal is so you can shoot from any angle or distance without looking up. If you hesitate on the ball, even for a split-second, a good scoring chance is often lost.

The golden rule of shooting is always to hit the target and force the goalkeeper into making a save. Shots on goal need power and accuracy if they are to beat the goalkeeper, but don't always rely on pure force, because even the fiercest of shots can be saved by a goalkeeper's outstretched leg, arm or foot. Remember, a goalkeeper also has instincts... for stopping the ball.

Goals can be scored with a number of different kicks, including gentle taps, chips, volleys or curling shots around the goalkeeper. These techniques and skills have been covered on pages 20–23.

Goals can also be scored by putting pressure on defenders and goalkeepers in the penalty area and seizing any opportunity to stab the ball into the net.

Basic techniques

Your team may create many goalscoring opportunities in a game, but fail to take advantage of any of them and you'll lose. To ensure you grab as many chances as possible you must simulate match conditions in practice by shooting with moving balls.

Shooting covers several kicking and passing techniques that have been explained on pages 20–23. The art of good shooting is to strike a balance between control, accuracy and power – and to be able to kick with both feet!

When shooting, position your

Balance, control, accuracy and power – the perfect shooting technique, as shown by Dunga of Brazil.

supporting foot alongside the ball with toes pointing in the direction you want it to go. With eyes firmly on the ball, keep your head and shoulders over the ball, using your arms for balance. Swing back the kicking leg with toes pointed outwards and then strike the ball in the middle with your instep. The kicking knee should be over the ball at the moment of impact to keep the shot low. With your head down and toes tensed and pointed, follow through with the kicking leg, adding power from the knee. If the ball has been struck with great power the force should lift your body off the ground.

If the ball is moving away from you as you are about to shoot, place your kicking foot ahead of it and strike with your toes pointed and tensed.

Shooting from a distance

You need to be able to kick with great power and be aware of the situation around you to shoot from long range. Always consider passing the ball to a team-mate who is in a better position to score than you are. Also be aware of the goalkeeper's position – a surprise shot from outside the area could catch him and the opposing defenders off guard.

For maximum power, the non-kicking foot should be alongside

Soccer Practice

Use a wall to practise shooting and ball control. Mark out targets and use both feet when kicking. Start by standing four to five yards from the wall, gradually increasing the distance between you and the wall. See how many times you can hit the target in a minute.

Get two players to stand on either side of the penalty-area and take it in turns to fire balls towards the penalty spot at all angles and heights for a third player to run on to and kick while they are moving. If no goalkeeper is available, shoot at a wall.

During five-a-side games, or training occasionally, try not to use your good foot. If you are naturally right-footed, play the ball with your left. Or play with a football boot on your weak foot and a softer training shoe on your strong foot.

Practise volleying by getting a friend to throw the ball towards the penalty-spot for you to strike before it hits the ground. When you have improved get another player to act as a defender and run from behind you and try to get the ball before you can kick it. This gets you used to being under pressure and helps speed up your reactions.

For chip shots, place a number of balls on the edge of the penalty area and see how many times you can hit the crossbar with them.

For a long-distance shot make sure the non-kicking foot is alongside the ball. Use the arms for balance and kick with the top of the foot, and then follow through.

Attacker (A) shoots for a goal. If the shot is pushed out by the goalkeeper or strikes the far post the ball could rebound to attackers (B) or (C).

Brazil's Bebeto side-foots to score from close range against the USA in World Cup '94.

the ball with your head over the ball. Arms should be outstretched to the side for balance. The ball should be struck with the top of the foot not with the toes, keep them down. Remember, keep your eyes on the ball and follow through with the kicking leg after making contact with the ball.

Your head must be down over the ball in order to keep the shot close to the ground. Low shots, particularly when aimed at the corners of the goal, are more difficult for the goalkeeper to deal with than a high shot directed just under the crossbar.

The great Dutch international star Ronald Koeman is famous for his long-rage shooting. It was his tremendous, thunderous 25-yard (23m) drive from a free kick that won the European Cup for Barcelona against Sampadoria at Wembley in 1992. Another long-range expert is Brazil's Branco.

Shooting from close range

England's former striker Gary Lineker scored many goals by pure instinct

When shooting from the edge of the penalty area, always aim just inside the far post.

Most goals are scored from this space within the penalty area marked by the dotted red line.

and reflex action from inside the six-yard (5.5m) box. Anticipation and accuracy are more important than power in close-range situations. Always be on the look-out for rebounds, stay alert and be ready to pounce on the loose ball and gently tap, or side-foot the ball into the net.

Positioning in the penalty area

Most goals are scored from an area that extends from the goalline to the penalty spot (above). The best area for scoring goals is seen by drawing a line from the goalposts to the edge of the penalty area, as shown in the diagram below. Inside the blue area you should pass the ball to a team-mate who might be better positioned. Inside the red area shoot for goal!

While play is inside the penalty area, be aware of what's happening around you and get into a position to snap up balls that have rebounded off posts, defenders' legs, or been parried by the goalkeeper. However, don't get caught offside! If a shot misses the target and flies across the goal, a player running in at the far post will have a good chance of reaching the ball and scoring.

Way-To-Play Tips

Eyes on the ball
It's important to keep your eyes firmly on the ball when making contact with it. Before you strike the ball, look to see where the goalkeeper is. You can take advantage of a badly-positioned goalkeeper.

Don't be afraid to miss
When shooting from long range don't be afraid of missing. If you are nervous you will lack confidence which will probably affect your accuracy.

Don't always aim for the centre of the goal. Pick a target such as the far post, or corner of the goal – vulnerable spots for goalkeepers.

Always follow up shots and make sure the ball has crossed the line if you are in any doubt.

Never change your mind as you prepare to shoot. He who hesitates loses.

Practise shooting with a good goalkeeper whenever possible. You won't learn anything, or get any real benefit out of taking shots at an outfield player who knows very little about stopping the ball.

– – – – Go for a goal in this area.
= = = = Inside this area pass the ball.

③ TRAPPING THE BALL

IF you are to play the game well, skilled trapping and controlling the football must become second nature. When you receive the ball your first touch must be a good one, especially if you are tightly marked. You must be able to stop the ball dead and bring it under control, often under pressure in a crowded area of the field.

A good first touch gives you space and time to make the next move – a pass, negotiate opponents, a shot for goal – or it lets you shield the ball with your body to hold off a challenge until you're able to make a positive move.

You will become an accomplished team player with mastery of ball control. Without, opposing players will find it easy to mark you tightly, giving them the initiative to take the ball from you.

Basic technique

Whichever part of the body is used to control or trap the ball the basic technique is the same. Keep your eyes firmly on the ball and get your body into the line of flight, so you are perfectly balanced and ready to take it in your stride. At the moment of impact, relax the part of the body you are using to control the ball. This movement acts as a cushion and slows down the ball, making it easier to control, whereas a rigid leg, foot, chest or head acts as a firm barrier off which the ball will bounce away from you.

Be positive and aware of how you're going to trap the ball and position your body accordingly, especially if you're being tightly marked by an opponent.

Trapping the ball with the inside of the foot

Keep your eyes on the ball, with your balancing foot firmly on the ground. Use the raised foot making contact with the ball to absorb, or cushion, its power by pulling the foot back slightly at the moment of impact. The ball should drop to the ground after hitting

the leg, making it easy to control with the inside of your foot. You are then ready to move away with the ball, or pass to a team-mate.

The trapping foot should be relaxed to cushion the ball. The more pace you can take off the ball, the easier it

Trapping the ball with the inside of the foot (top) and the outside (bottom).

is to control. Keep your balance so that you can move quickly away with the ball. Timing is also important, or the ball could bounce away from you.

Trapping with the outside of the foot

To trap the ball with the outside of your foot, lean your body towards the ball's flight. At the moment of impact the foot should be relaxed and the knee slightly bent to cushion and slow down the ball's pace. If you are about to be challenged, keep your supporting leg between the ball and your opponent. This helps to retain your balance and shield the ball from a challenger.

You should now be ideally placed to pass to a team-mate, or go around an opponent. If you are being marked, your opponent will find it difficult to tackle and get the ball from you without committing a foul.

Chest traps

When a high ball is falling, a player may not be able to wait for it to reach the ground before trapping and getting it under control. In this situation the chest trap is the answer. Often high balls crossed into the penalty area have to be controlled at chest height before a striker is in a position to shoot for goal. An experienced defender also deflects balls away from danger by turning the chest as the ball hits it, but you should always try to head the ball clear.

To perform the chest trap you must keep your eyes on the ball, get your body in line with its flight as it comes towards you, and correct your balance by using your arms. Watching the ball closely as it continues to drop, bend your knees slightly and extend your arms. You should be on your toes and leaning back slightly as the ball makes contact with your chest. Try to cushion the impact by relaxing your chest muscles and lean your head over the ball as it falls to your feet. Great defenders such as Steve Bruce, captain of the 1994 English Premier League Champions, Manchester United, have perfected the chest trap and often use it to deflect the ball to safety. In the

In a chest trap, the ball's impact is cushioned by leaning back and relaxing the chest muscles to bring the ball under control.

If the ball is falling towards you at an awkward angle, use the thigh trap to stop it and bring it under control.

Way-To-Play Tips

Cushion control
You can gain control of the ball more quickly and more effectively by taking the pace off it. As the ball hits your legs or chest, relax the muscles, bending your legs slightly on impact to cushion it.

One touch
Remember to control the ball with your first touch, and to pass or to take opponents on or shoot for goal with your second. This way you don't give opponents the opportunity to tackle you.

European Cup-Winners' Cup Final against Barcelona in 1991, Steve contributed to United's victory through clearing the danger on several occasions by pushing the ball away with his chest. He does this by tensing his chest at the moment of impact and twisting his body from the hips to send the ball in the direction he wants.

Thigh traps

The thigh is often used to control a ball that's dropping towards you at an awkward height when you're on the move. It can also be used to push the ball into the air to allow you to volley it with the other leg. The thigh control makes the ball drop to the feet quicker than the chest trap. Turn your body towards the ball, relax the thigh muscles and allow it to hit your thigh. Ensuring your supporting leg is slightly bent, let the ball drop to your feet, leaving you ready to pass, or quickly turn and lose your marker.

Soccer Practice

Make a triangle using three players. Trap and pass the ball between you. Keep the ball moving and pass over longer distances as you improve your control.

A simple solo exercise is to throw a ball into the air and trap it as it falls to the ground, using the inside of your foot.

One player passes to you when you're positioned inside the centre-circle. Trap the ball while being challenged by a third player and try to pass back to the first player, who runs around the edge of the centre-circle. Take it in turns to change position.

Find two walls at right angles. Kick the ball against one wall and when it comes back trap and hit it against the other wall. Use your feet and head in five- to ten-minute spells. Increase the times as you improve.

ONE of the most exciting sights in the game is to see a player go on a run and dribble the ball past several opponents, while keeping it under close control. The player weaves one way then the other, evading tackle after tackle before using the developed pace to leave opponents stranded.

You might recall Diego Maradona's second goal for Argentina in the 1986 World Cup quarter-finals when he darted through the heart of England's defence – the ball appeared to be glued to his boot! Italy's World Cup star Roberto Baggio also possesses all the attributes needed to be a superb attacking player and is a prime example for all young players to watch and to try to emulate.

Always remember, though, soccer is a team game, dribbling past three or four defenders and then losing the ball

Italy's Roberto Baggio is well balanced as he sprints into space with the ball.

to a fifth who starts a dangerous counter-attack is no good to your team. Dribbling and running with the ball are most effective on the wings, especially against tight defences.

Once near the goalline you can cross the ball to team-mates positioned in front of the goal. Defenders forced into a tackle are often left stranded, or have to concede a corner.

To have good dribbling skills you need ball control, balance, pace, and quick reactions in one-on-one situations.

Running with the ball to get away from opponents and move into space requires pace, close control and an awareness of the players around you. When you're running with the ball look around to spot opponents who appear set to challenge you, or team-mates who are in good positions to receive your pass.

Basic technique

When dribbling a ball, think of it as part of your foot. Lean over the ball and keep it within comfortable distance, close enough to control but with space to let you move away, or change direction if you are challenged. Look to see how your opponent is standing. If he's flat-footed, instead of on his toes, he will be slow off the mark when challenging or chasing you.

When running with the ball, push it slightly ahead. The faster you run the further you can push the ball. Try to combine pace and balance with a body-swerve and a dip of the shoulder to confuse your opponent about your intended direction.

Keeping the ball on the blindside

When you're in possession of the ball and are being closely marked you may have to move forward, or (more often than not) keep the ball until you're in a better position to release it. Protect or shield the ball from an opponent by keeping your body between the two, preventing your opponent from seeing, or reaching the ball.

With your head leaning forwards, put your weight on the non-kicking foot. Hold your arms out slightly behind your body. This helps your balance and makes it difficult for your opponent to tackle.

Run with the ball as the opponent

moves in to tackle from the side. As you're challenged from the left, control the ball with the outside of your right foot, or the outside of your left foot if challenged from the right.

Twist and turn your back to your opponent and use a body swerve, or dummy to move away with the ball on the opponent's blind side.

Change of pace

Move towards an opponent at your normal speed but when you close drop a shoulder and veer away, slightly stepping up the pace until you are sprinting away with the ball.

If the opponent runs alongside you, slow down and then suddenly pick up the pace again to leave him stranded. You can also wrong-foot opponents by pretending to stop the ball with the sole of your foot and dragging it in the same direction, accelerating away.

Swerving

This is a simple way to wrong-foot a defender. Drop a shoulder and look as if you intend to go off in one direction, for example to the right. As your opponent moves to the right to cover, swerve your body and pass on the left. If you carry this out correctly, the defender gets caught off-balance and cannot recover in time to challenge.

Feinting

One of the simplest ways (but often the most impressive to watch) of catching an opponent off-balance is by pretending to play the ball in one direction, but then play it the opposite way. As an opponent moves to challenge, make a kicking motion. At the last second check the foot's kick and drag or push the ball in another direction.

In a match situation a player may feint to kick the ball hard, but instead suddenly swivels on the standing foot and turns the ball with the inside of the playing foot behind the standing leg.

Another good dummy, or feint, is to run with the ball and pretend to push it along with the outside of the foot, but instead pass the foot over the ball and drag it forwards with the

Brazil's Romario running with the ball displays both pace and close control

Way-To-Play Tips

Don't get mugged
Do not dribble the ball in your own penalty area. You could easily lose possession.

Speed is important, but so is close control. Regulate your pace to ensure you keep possession of the ball.

Do not use the same foot when dribbling. Juggle the ball from foot to foot, also varying your speed to keep opponents guessing.

Try not to get pushed out wide, or take on one opponent too many. Always look for the opportunity to catch out opponents by passing to a team-mate.

Call a team-mate by name as if you are going to pass. This diverts your opponent's attention long enough for you to take the ball past.

Look up and be aware of the players around you.

Soccer Practice

Set up a row of cones, garden sticks, or plastic bottles about six yards (5.5m) apart. Weave in and out of the cones with a ball, using the inside and outside of the foot. When you have reached the end of the obstacles, stop the ball with the sole of your boot, turn and go in the other direction. Time yourself and try to beat your best time.

You can use this exercise on your own, or with a friend. If there are two of you, pass the ball to your partner once you have reached the end of the course. The partner plays the ball back to you so that you have to control it before setting off down the course again.

Five players acting as forwards stand in a position about 12–15 yards (10–13m) outside the penalty area. Each is confronted by a defender standing just inside the area. Each attacker then runs at their respective opponent trying to dribble past into the area and shoot for goal. After an agreed amount of time the defenders change places with the attackers.

inside of the other foot. Slow down, then accelerate as you play the ball with the inside of your foot.

Evading a tackle

Be extremely careful when on the ball because a defender attempting to tackle you can, even accidentally, give you a very nasty injury if he kicks you. As he lunges for the ball make sure neither you nor the ball are in the way.

ONCE you can control the ball you need to learn about distribution – the art of keeping possession by linking with team-mates through good, accurate passes. Passes can be made with the head or feet, on the ground or in the air, over long and short distances. You can even use your hands. A throw-in is a pass, and so is a throw-out by a goalkeeper.

Accurate passing of the ball is a skill. England's Paul Gascoigne when at his best is a tremendous distributor of the ball, especially in tight situations. Other good examples are Germany's star Lothar Matthäus and Enzo Scifo of Belgium.

When you're about to pass the ball you must care-fully consider a number of possibilities before releasing it. If the ball is struck too hard it is difficult for the receiver to control it. If the ball is not struck sufficiently hard it could fail to reach its target and be intercepted by an opponent. If the ball is kicked into space for a team-mate to run on to, your team could lose possession.

It is also important to look up when you are about to release the ball to see exactly where your team-mates and opponents are. Like Gascoigne, Matthäus and Scifo, good passers need control of the ball, accuracy, good balance and an awareness of the situation to ensure they don't give the ball away.

Basic technique

To pass accurately you have to be able to kick the ball well and with confidence, using the inside, outside or instep of your foot (or feet!). When passing, keep your eyes on the ball at the moment of impact, and use your arms for balance. Strike the ball in its middle for low passes. Strike it just below the centre line for long, lofted passes. Follow through with the kicking foot in a deliberate, smooth action and with the non-kicking foot pointed in the direction you want the ball to go.

The side-foot or push pass

This is the most common, and most accurate way of passing to a team-mate along the ground over a short distance. Your non-kicking foot should be on the ground alongside the ball. Look at the team-mate you are about to pass to, then strike the ball in the centre with the inside of

Soccer Practice

Playing in twos is an excellent way to practise basic passing, and to perfect that all-important accuracy at speed. Here are some handy training tips:

Stand parallel to a team-mate about four to five yards (4–5m) apart. Run up and down the pitch keeping your distance and passing the ball to each other. Each pass is made slightly ahead of the receiver so he can take the ball and play it in his stride. The receiver controls the ball using the inside of the far foot and passes it back in the next stride with the same foot. Repeat the exercise over a ten-minute spell, gradually increasing the distance between you and your partner.

A good training exercise for four or more players involves interpassing in a triangular formation. Three players (A, B and C) pass to each other in a triangle. The ball is passed between any one of them and (D), who is continuing on the move and returns the ball to any one of the three players. They should remain alert in anticipation of (D) making a pass. Switch positions around after a few minutes.

your foot, keeping your body over the ball. Swing through with a pendulum movement from the hip to complete the pass.

The long pass

As with the push pass, your non-kicking foot must be alongside the ball and pointing towards the player about to receive it. Use the instep to make the ball rise into the air. Keeping your ankle firm, lift back the kicking foot with toes pointed towards the ground and aim to strike the ball below the centre line. As you strike the ball lean back and follow through to ensure it is hit with power.

The Wall Pass

Under pressure or if you're closely marked, the wall pass – also known as a return pass – is useful. With the inside of your foot pass to a team-mate who has moved away at an angle to you. As the team-mate collects the ball, move away on the marker's blind side to accept a quick return pass in your stride, leaving your opponent stranded. In a sense, you have used your team-mate as a wall to bounce the ball off. This is also known as the 'one-two'.

Running off the ball

There is no use passing the ball unless you have a team-mate to pass it to. Successful moves and build-ups rely on unmarked players being in positions to receive the ball when they have run into space. They should then have time to control the ball and pass it on before being challenged. All good players have the vision to move into space to avoid being marked. Timing the run is vital – move too soon and you could find yourself offside or under heavy pressure when the pass is made to you.

Way-To-Play Tips

Pass and run
After delivering a pass to a team-mate, run into space to support him and be ready to take a return pass. Many teams base their game on this simple tactic.

Make it tough for defenders
Try to keep yourself between the defender and the ball when passing to make a challenge difficult to deliver.

On the move
Always run into space when you haven't got the ball. You will be much more difficult to mark and you'll be in a position to receive a pass without being challenged.

Foot talk
Remember the instep is used to achieve power, the inside of the foot for accuracy and the outside of the foot to swerve the ball and catch your opponent off-guard. The stronger and straighter the follow-through, the greater the power and accuracy.

INSET shows the side-foot, or push pass, where the ball is struck in the centre with the inside of the foot, directing it accurately towards a team-mate.

Power and accuracy are vital to the long pass. Note how the player's non-kicking foot is placed alongside the ball to help the shot's aim. The ball is kicked just below its centre to loft it; the follow-through provides the power.

6 TACKLING

FLUID PASSING, scorching shooting and nifty ball-control all look great, but to achieve them you have to have the ball! This is where the less glamorous but vital art of tackling is paramount.

Often to win the ball you must tackle an opponent. A good tackle is a hard but fair challenge on the player with the ball. Like passing, shooting and dribbling, tackling requires skill and technique. Expert tacklers not only win the ball, but can set up a counter-attack immediately after. Italian international star Paolo Maldini is one of the world's top defenders. He's very strong in the tackle but is also a superb reader of the game. Once he's won the ball his distribution is top class. England midfielder Paul Ince is also a brilliant winner and distributor of the ball.

But tackling does not only concern defenders or ball-winning midfielders. Every player on the field, including the goalkeeper, should learn and practise the art of winning the ball cleanly. There are three basic methods of tackling an opponent: the front block; the side block; and the sliding tackle.

Basic technique

Don't look at your opponent. Keep your eyes on the ball and use the side of your foot to make contact with it. Challenge for the ball when you are confident of winning it. Timing is vital to avoid missing the ball and striking your opponent. Clumsy challenges will be penalised by the referee, so be accurate. Put the whole of your leg and weight into the tackle and go in with determination. Hesitation, or relaxing your body, could result in your opponent brushing you aside or you could suffer a serious injury.

It's worth remembering that certain methods of tackling are determined by a defender's position or attacking line of approach by an opponent.

The front block tackle

This is the strongest form of tackling. It is used when two players going for the ball reach it at the same time. It's also known in the game as going for a 50/50 ball. As your opponent tries to play the ball, close in and use the

In a 50/50 ball situation, the front block tackle is the most powerful means of gaining possession. The inside of the foot is used to block the ball, and then scoop it away from the challenger. In all tackling situations, look at the ball, not at your opponent.

Use the side block tackle to take the ball off an opponent running in the same direction as yourself.

side of your foot to block the ball firmly. When you've made contact with the ball, ensure your body weight is on the tackling leg. Leaning a shoulder towards your opponent adds strength to your challenge.

The side block tackle

The side block tackle is used to take the ball off an opponent running in the same direction as yourself. When tackling an opponent from an angle, or the side, you must put all your weight on the tackling leg and slightly bend your supporting leg. As you make contact with the ball, turn and lean forwards in the direction of the tackle.

The slide tackle

The aim of the sliding tackle is not so much to gain possession of the ball, but to deflect it away from your

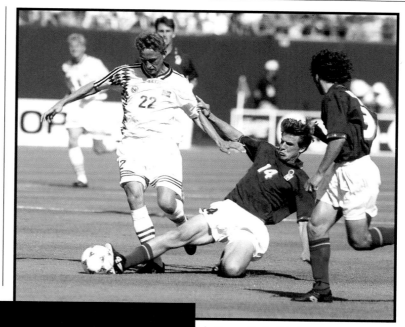

The perfect slide tackle require split-second timing. Here, Nicola Berti of Italy tackles Norway's Lars Bohinen during the 1994 World Cup.

Soccer Practice

Use a small pitch with four attackers against three defenders marking one-on-one. Throughout the game the spare attacker is only allowed to receive the ball from a back pass.

Mark out a small area 10 yards (9m) square, or use the penalty area. Use three players. One tries to win the ball, while the other two pass it between them. Take it in turns to be the attacker.

Stand as a pair facing each other one stride from the ball. Both of you place the left foot slightly behind and to the side of the ball. Then, using the right foot, make a block tackle at the ball. Increase the power of the tackle and switch to the other foot after a ten-minute spell.

One player runs down the pitch in a straight line with the ball. After five yards (4.5m) another player runs in pursuit and attempts to gain possession of the ball with a fair slide tackle from behind, hooking the ball away with the attacking foot.

Set up two cones six yards (5.5m) apart. Player (A) stands between the cones while two others, (B and C), position themselves on either side ten yards (9m) away. Players (B) and (C) pass the ball to each other between the cones, while player (A) tries to intercept. This is a good defensive training exercise.

opponent to a team-mate, or safely out of play. This is a difficult tackling skill to perfect. To win the ball cleanly and not foul your opponent after committing yourself requires split-second timing.

Try to challenge for the ball with your stronger leg, aiming your foot slightly in front of it. Keeping your eyes firmly on the ball, bend your supporting leg and slide on the knee and shin of this leg, putting your weight behind the tackling foot – a straight arm helps support the body when the tackling foot stretches to play the ball. After deflecting, or blocking the ball, withdraw your foot to avoid tripping your opponent. Watch Brazilian defender Marcio Santos in action. No-one times the sliding tackle better, and he usually comes away with the ball.

The back-heel tackle

Get close to the player you intend tackling so that you are running side by side. With your eyes on the ball, raise the foot of the tackling leg and block the ball with your heel. Do not swing the leg backwards, but check as it makes contact with the ball, transferring your weight to the tackling foot.

The shoulder charge

Manoeuvre yourself into position by running alongside the player you are about to challenge. In a slightly crouching position, come shoulder to shoulder with your opponent, ensuring only your upper arm and shoulder makes contact and that the challenge is from the side, not behind.

When you make contact put all your weight into the shoulder and lean in with the supporting leg for balance. When your opponent is off-balance, use the side of the foot to attack and win the ball.

INSET: The bak-heel tackle is like a back-heel kick, but the aim is to block the ball. However, it is a dangerous tackle to try.

In the shoulder charge the challenge must be from the side, using only the upper arm and shoulder to make contact. The object is to unbalance your opponent so that you can use the side of the foot to capture the ball.

BELOW: Although the defender is going to get the ball in the tackle, the attacker will probably be brought down as he won't be able to lift his leg over the tackler. This should not be a foul, but it is a risky challenge.

Jockeying for position is a way of frustrating an opponent in possession of the ball and forcing him to make a mistake so that you can go in for a tackle.

Jockeying for position

You can stop an opponent in possession by jockeying, or closing him down, and set him up for a tackle. Approach your opponent when he has the ball under control, but keep your eyes on the ball. As the opponent moves towards you, back off slowly, leaving him as little space as possible to play the ball, or increase the pace of play. Keep your eyes on the ball and wait for a mistake or a turn. Some players are uncomfortable if they keep the ball too long. They get frustrated and take risks. When you feel confident of getting the ball, go firmly into the tackle. It is important to remain patient and stay on your feet.

Way-To-Play Tips

Perfect timing
Timing is essential. Go in hard, but take the ball cleanly. A mistimed tackle can result in a foul and a free kick or penalty kick being awarded against you as well as getting a yellow or red card.

Confidence and determination
Always believe you are going to win the ball. Go in half-heartedly and you'll be pushed aside, or risk injury.

Tackle in training
Don't hold off tackling during training or five-a-side games. Some teams do this to avoid injuries. But you play as you train. If you stop tackling in training defenders can develop a bad habit of holding off or hesitating during a game, while forwards can get a false sense of security when in possession.

Stand-up
Don't dive in when tackling. Stay on your feet. You can't tackle effectively on the ground.

Side on
The frontal stance – presenting most of your body to an opponent you're about to take on – is the best tackling method for young players. But when you gain experience, try experimenting with a diagonal stance. This forces moves in other directions and so makes opponents less confident on the ball.

7 HEADING THE BALL

HEADING the ball is a vital facet of the game. It's also one of the most difficult skills to perfect. The most common fault among young players learning to head a football is fear – they are afraid of not connecting with the ball properly and getting hurt as a result.

Because it is not a natural action, it's unsurprising that you may reflexively close your eyes when heading the ball. The result is that you head the ball with the top of your head and not the forehead. Because the reflex action to close your eyes when an object approaches is natural, you shouldn't be ashamed of it. But conquering it is essential if you want to be a better player.

As with all techniques covered in this book, it is important to practise this skill until you are comfortable heading the ball. Although the techniques used to head the ball under different circumstances are similar, there are four distinct types of header: attacking; defensive; glancing; and cushion (or head trap).

Basic technique

Whatever type of header you perform, they all require confidence and perfect timing. Apart from the glancing header, the ball should be met with the forehead. This is the strongest part of the skull and is much harder and tougher than a football. By using your forehead, the eyes can follow the ball right to the moment of impact.

That's the theory behind heading, but what's it like in practice? It's important to keep your eyes on the ball as it ball drops towards you and to concentrate on directing the ball to the intended target. As the ball approaches, tense your neck muscles and move your head slightly back. To help you achieve a good contact, try imagining that you have a target painted on your forehead. When the ball comes into range, aim to meet it where the bullseye would be.

When you make contact with the ball, thrust your forehead forwards sharply. Follow through with your body, bending your elbows back to

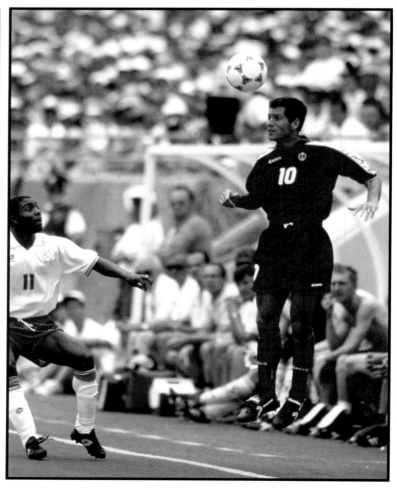

Belgium's Enzo Scifo (10) heads the ball away from Holland's Bryan Roy.

Soccer Practice

In threes: the players stand in a triangular formation about five yards (4.5m) apart. (A) throws the ball to (B), who heads the ball on to (C). (C) fields the ball, throws it to (A) who heads it to (B), and so on...

In pairs: Stand 12 yards (11m) apart. Throw the ball so that your partner can make a standing jump to head it back. Alternatively, stand 15 yards (13.7m) apart. Throw the ball so that your partner can run forward and jump to head it back.

Heading Volley Ball

Two six-a-side teams compete in heading the ball over a net seven feet high (2m) without letting the ball touch the ground. The ball is served by a player from the base-line of the court, striking it by hand to send it over the net. The ball is then headed back and forth over the net. If it drops to the ground, fails to go over the net, or goes out of play, the service or the point is lost to the other side. This game is particularly suited to indoor arenas.

take advantage should the goalkeeper be poorly positioned. If the goalkeeper is off-balance when leaping to catch the ball, the attacker has a distinct advantage.

England captain David Platt has often proved a matchwinner for club and country by timing his runs to arrive late in the penalty-area and score with an attacking header. Germany's World Cup star Rudi Völler is also a great exponent of the attacking header.

Heading for goal

This may seems obvious, but it is worth remembering that if you head the ball downwards you have a high-

help add more power to the header. This action gives the ball its impetus and, if your technique is good, should prevent you from getting hurt.

Cushion headers require less power than standard headers but the technique up until the moment of contact is the same. If you have to jump for the ball it is better to run forwards to meet it than wait for it to hit you. Leap into the air with your leading leg while running, since this gives you greater height than a standing two-footed jump. A word of caution, remember to keep your arms down when jumping. You don't need to use your elbows for leverage, and jumping at an opponent is a foul.

Attacking headers

The aim of the attacking header is to create havoc in the opposing penalty area and, hopefully, score. This header, like a shot at goal, should be aimed low, because it is the toughest attack for goalkeepers to save. When heading a crossed ball, be ready to

HEADING: keep your eyes on the ball, sway back, then bring the head forwards and follow through with a strong punch.

Mark Hughes attacks the ball with his head, achieving great power and accuracy.

goals. They are also very hard to defend against. A diving header can also help a defender protect his goal, or clear his lines.

The technique used to perform the diving header is essentially the same as that used for other headers, but there are three important points to stress:

(1) throw your arms out in front, below the height of your shoulders, to add power to your dive;

2) make contact with your forehead and not the top of the head;

3) bend your knees and relax your arms to help cushion your fall.

Defensive headers

Defenders must be able to head the ball powerfully and accurately when the team is under pressure. And they must be strong enough to reach it before an opponent, especially in a crowded penalty area.

Don't wait for the ball to drop when heading in defence – attack it as it arrives, jumping and striking the ball with the middle of your forehead. Don't worry about opponents. Pay too much attention to them instead of the ball, and you'll lose concentration.

Jumping for the ball

Lean forwards to gain height as you jump. Before heading the ball, arch your back and flex your neck and shoulder muscles. When you're in the air try to hit the ball at the highest point of your jump. Make contact with the centre of the ball and hammer your head and neck forward in one movement to add power to the header.

percentage chance of hitting the target rather than ballooning the ball over the crossbar. This is the main reason why defenders head the ball up while attackers head down.

The vast majority of headers on goal come from either crosses or other glanced headers (which are discussed later). In a crowded penalty area positioning is vital. When launching yourself at the ball be aware of the location of your opponents, the goalkeeper and, most importantly, the goal.

If you're outside the penalty area, judge the flight of the ball, run, jump

and head it towards the point you calculate will take it in front of goal.

When heading from a cross, steer the ball back in the direction from which it came, aiming for the near post. If you use this method there's a good chance the goalkeeper may be unsighted and out of position. And don't forget the golden rule: headers aimed downwards are much more accurate than balls headed in the air.

Diving headers

Diving headers, when attacking players dive full length to head a low cross, often result in spectacular

With the diving header, make sure that your arms are well forward and the knees bent for a softer fall.

Way-To-Play Tips

Eye on the ball
Remember, once you have decided to go for a header don't change your mind! Attack the ball by getting in front of your opponent. Watch the ball right up to the moment of impact.

Don't duck
Do not head the ball if it is below your waist (except for diving headers) – you might get kicked in the face by an opponent.

Time your jumps
Good heading usually involves jumping. A well-timed leap helps you with high balls and gives you a big advantage over your opponents.

Backwards danger
Avoid heading the ball when running backwards. You will not be able to jump for the ball, or generate enough power or control over your header.

To get the required power and height into a jump, good timing is essential. Even a short run up and a single-foot take-off will give you greater height than you can achieve by making a standing jump with both feet.

In defence, if you're covering an opponent from behind and you need to jump vertically for a high ball, you should stand slightly away from the player you are marking. This gives you space to run forwards when making a jump for the ball. It also prevents you from making bodily contact with your opponent and committing a foul.

The glancing header

The forehead is used to deflect the ball in different directions when performing a glancing header (or flick-on). Remember, you can use the force of the ball to redirect it away from an opponent, or towards the goal. The forehead acts as a block, or gliding surface, off which to bounce the ball.

When you've made contact with the ball, twist your head and body in the direction you want it to go. The harder you strike the ball with your forehead, the more power and pace your glancing header will have. This can prove decisive in front of goal.

With the glancing header, also referred to as 'deflecting the ball', use your head and body to glance the ball in the desired direction.

ESSENTIALLY, a throw-in is a method of restarting play. But in the modern game it is also used as a tactical weapon to create scoring chances, and in this respect it is an important skill to perfect.

Taking a throw-in ought to be easy, especially as there are 20–40 awarded during every match. Despite this frequency, it's amazing how many players commit foul throws and so give the advantage to the opposition.

Before playing, assign players in your team to take the throw-ins. Confusion over who is going to take a throw-in can lose vital seconds, while the opposition can regroup. The last thing a coach wants to see is team-mates arguing among themselves over who is to take

a throw-in – and conversely you don't need the team confused because no-one steps forward to take the throw.

If you are going to call for the ball from a throw-in you should always move around. The more space you can create, the more difficult you are to mark and close down. And when you are throwing in select a team-mate to throw at, or throw the ball into space for your selected team-mate to run on to. Don't just throw the ball in the general direction of a team-mate – ensure the person you select knows what your intentions are.

It's useful to remember that if you receive a ball from a throw-in when you're in an attacking position you cannot be offside.

Basic technique

Stand with both feet on or behind the touchline at the point where the ball went out of play when taking a throw-in. Both hands must be on the ball as you throw from behind and over your head. You may raise your heels but a part of each foot must remain firmly on the ground. When throwing the ball, it is advisable to stand just behind the touchline. This helps you avoid putting one, or both feet on to the Field Of Play.

The long throw

This can be a useful attacking option anywhere within 30 yards (27.5m) of your opponent's penalty-area and can be as effective as a corner kick. The long throw is used prominently in the British game. In the rest of the world and at international level, teams usually rely on the short, quick throw.

Wimbledon and Wales defender Vinny Jones, often criticised for his

Soccer Practice

In pairs: one player sits down, the other stands up five yards (4.5m) away. The standing player throws the ball to the sitting player who catches it and throws it back from behind the head.

In pairs: stand with feet astride, ten yards (9m) apart. Throw a ball overhead to each other. After a few minutes do the same but with one foot forwards. This enables you to put more pace on the ball.

In pairs: your partner throws a ball to you. Control it with your head, chest or feet before kicking it back. If the ball bounces before reaching the partner, switch roles.

Safety in the defensive third of the field is vital. With his team-mates marked, full back (A) has room to clear the throw-in from player (B).

'over-enthusiastic tackling', is an expert at the long throw into opponent's danger areas.

For long throws, the hands should be placed behind the ball (not on the side as for a normal throw-in) to give

In the long throw-in, the hands should be placed behind the ball to provide more power. Lean well back with one leg extended behind the throw, but still ensuring both feet remain on the ground and on or behind the touchline.

Way-To-Play Tips

Don't let the ball bounce
Throw the ball to the receiver's head, chest or feet – don't throw it in front of him, unless it is downfield for him to run onto. If the ball bounces it will be more difficult to control.

Dummy runs
If you are about to receive the ball from a throw-in, move as if you are going to run in one direction, but then quickly switch and move in another. Your marker will be caught off-guard and you'll create extra space to receive the ball from the thrower.

Concentrate
Always concentrate on the basics. Lifting a foot, or failing to take the ball behind the head results in a foul throw – why make it easy for the opposition to gain possession?

Quick return
You can retain possession if the receiver plays the ball straight back to the player who has just taken the throw-in.

it extra power, height and distance. Lean back as far as you can, remembering to keep both feet on the ground behind the touchline, and lift your heels off the ground. Tense your stomach muscles and heave your body forwards, swinging the arms powerfully over your head. With a final flick of the fingers, propel the ball high into the danger-zone.

The long throw-in can also be used by defenders to throw the ball back to the goalkeeper, or down the touchline for an attacking team-mate to run onto.

Strong stomach muscles and powerful shoulders are essential to achieve an effective long throw-in.

The short, quick throw-in

A short throw-in taken quickly can be just as effective as a long throw. It is used to get the ball back into play, to keep possession, set up attacking opportunities and catch opponents off guard.

9 GOALKEEPING

THERE'S an old saying in the game that 'you have to be crazy to be a goal-keeper'. Whether that's true or not is a matter of opinion, but you certainly do need to be a different character from the rest of the team.

Goalkeeping is a highly specialised role, demanding specialist skills. This is the most important member of the team, playing in the most demanding and difficult position of all. They are under constant pressure to play well because the slightest mistake can be cruelly punished and result in a goal being scored, or even worse, defeat. Outfield players can afford to have an off day, make the occasional mistake, misplaced pass, or shoot wide of the target. But not goalkeepers.

Good goalkeeping is an art and many leading professional clubs employ ex-keepers as coaches to pass on their knowledge and experience.

Denmark's ace goalkeeper Peter Schmeichel takes the ball off Germany's Jürgen Klinsmann in 1992's European Championship Final.

A goalkeeper should be tall, with strong hands and shoulders. He needs to possess the agility of a gymnast, the reflexes of a tennis star, the strength and courage of a rugby forward and the ball-handling skills of a basketball player. The best keepers are also commanding and aggressive on the field with an unflappable temperament. It requires someone who can keep his emotions under control if he has made a mistake and not allow it to affect his team-mates. A temperamental keeper can be a liability because anger and frustration will unsettle the defenders in front of him.

But an extrovert keeper's antics can be positive. The Zimbabwe international goalkeeper Bruce Grobbelaar is renowned for his handstands and famous wobbly-knees act to distract A.S. Roma penalty takers in the 1984 European Cup Final. Peter Schmeichel, Denmark's extrovert goalkeeper, who remains unflappable in his own box, is also famous for joining his team's attack at a corner if they are losing late in an important game.

Another of the most extrovert goalkeepers in recent years is Colombia's Rene Higuita. He often comes out of his goal to dribble the ball down the wing, or tackle an opponent outside his penalty area. He operates like a spare sweeper. But he lived too dangerously during the 1990 World Cup finals against Cameroon when he lost the ball to Roger Milla, who went on to score.

In the modern game, as a goalkeeper you are required to do more than just stop shots. The position provides an excellent view of the game and you must have the vision to create moves by distributing the ball, by feet, or hand to team-mates in good strategic positions.

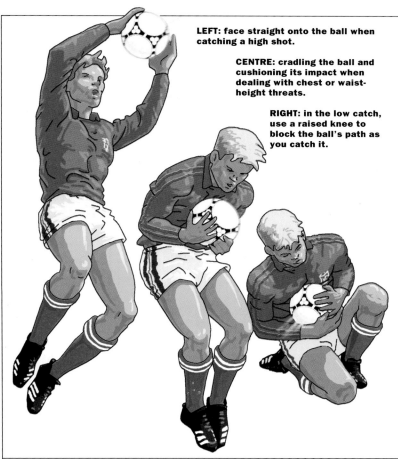

LEFT: face straight onto the ball when catching a high shot.

CENTRE: cradling the ball and cushioning its impact when dealing with chest or waist-height threats.

RIGHT: in the low catch, use a raised knee to block the ball's path as you catch it.

Basic technique

The basic principle of goalkeeping is safety first. This means getting both hands on the ball, with the body behind the hands to form a second barrier. Keeping balanced is most important but your position varies with the height, speed and direction of the ball as it comes to you. This goes not only for your body and legs but also for your arms and hands.

Stopping a ground shot

There are two ways of stopping a shot fired along the ground. The stooping catch and the kneeling gather. For the stoop, make sure you are in direct line with the flight of the ball. Keep your legs straight and bend down at the waist. Place the hands and palms upwards with the little fingers together under the ball and scoop the ball firmly upwards into the chest, grasping it tightly with both hands.

To gather a shot in the kneeling position, move the lower half of the body and feet sideways into line with the ball. Lower one knee to the ground, level with the opposite heel, and turn your chest towards the ball to form a wider barrier. Keeping your head steady and eyes on the ball, scoop the ball into the chest as before.

Catching the ball at waist height

When stopping shots at waist height, the whole body should be behind the line of the ball, with the palms of the hands pointed upwards so the ball can be scooped and gathered safely into the chest, which should be relaxed on impact to cushion the power of the shot. Wrap your hands around the ball and bend your chest forwards over it. This helps prevent the ball slipping out of your grasp.

Catching the ball at chest height

To prevent the ball bouncing off your chest when catching it, place both hands behind it when making contact. The elbows should be kept close to the body and the fingers outspread.

Catching the ball above the head

Dealing with high balls and crosses is probably the most important aspect of your goalkeeper's role after stopping shots. You have a distinct advantage over your opponents because you can use your hands, and will be already on the move as the ball comes across enabling you to jump much higher.

You should try to take the ball at its highest point and not wait for it to drop. Get into position using short steps and carefully watching the flight of the ball, take off with a spring, getting your arms up early and high, with both hands behind the ball and fingers outspread. After catching the ball firmly with hands

Way-To-Play Tips

Body behind the ball

Make sure you're fully behind the ball by moving your body and feet before getting your hands into position. Once your feet are in position, the body naturally follows.

Concentrate!

Retain concentration for the whole game. You could go for 88 minutes without having a shot to save and then, in the 89th minute, have to deal with an attacker running at you, or a dangerous high cross. Think positively all the time and don't be distracted.

the ball is coming straight at you. With clenched fists make contact with the centre of the ball and send it back in the direction it came from.

When using one fist, use the arm nearest the goal line and don't swing at the ball. The punching action should again be as straight as possible. Make sure you punch with the knuckle and aim to fist the ball as high in the air as possible. If you punch the ball out at head height, or below, the ball could drop to an opponent in a good scoring position.

On occasions during a game you may not be sure of getting two hands on the ball and may prefer to palm or deflect it over the crossbar. Leap as if to catch the ball, but with a natural overarm swing, spread the palm and fingers to make a good contact and guide it over the crossbar. Be ready to stretch your arm and finger tips and dive full length if the shot is particularly powerful, or at an angle. You should aim to reach the ball

before it drops below the level of the crossbar, but if the shot is dipping below the bar two hands might be needed. Time your jump to give an upwards thrust to the hands which should be close together and bent slightly backwards.

To deflect a ball around a post, follow the flight right on to the palm of your hand. Tense your wrist at the moment of impact to cushion the power of the ball and guide it around the upright.

Diving at a striker's feet

Timing is crucial to good handling, especially when diving at an attacker's feet in a one-against-one situation to smother the ball with the body. Courage is part of a goalkeeper's job, and a great deal of it is needed when diving at the feet of an opponent who's broken through into the area. Injuries can occur if a keeper hesitates, or uses the wrong technique.

As you come out to face your

wrapped around it, clutch it to your chest, protecting it as you hit the ground. This helps you hold on to the ball if an opponent makes a challenge, or crashes into you.

Punching and deflecting the ball

There are times when a goalkeeper under pressure in a crowded penalty area or goalmouth, is forced to punch the ball away, deflect it over the crossbar, or around a post.

Because of their vulnerability against tall attackers, smaller goalkeepers may prefer to punch the ball away when dealing with high crosses. A two-fisted punch is best used when

Smothering the ball: the body curls protectively around the ball. Keep your head protected from a flying boot.

Crystal Palace keeper Nigel Martyn dives to punch the ball away.

attacker, get into a low position with knees bent, head and shoulders forward and arms in front of your head. Get as low to the ground as possible when going for the ball so that your body is a yard (1m) or so behind it. Make sure your timing is right. If you dive too soon the attacker can lift the ball over your body, dive too late and the ball could slip under your body. Also make sure your body is along the ground at an angle before reaching for the ball. Get your body as close to the ball as you can when grabbing it from the attacker's feet and clutching it into your chest. Your head should be protected as it is tucked behind your hands, arms and legs, well away from the ball.

Kicking the ball from your hands

Like all good outfield players, goalkeepers should be able to use both feet and have the strength to kick the ball half the length of the field.

Only being able to kick with one foot can be a great tactical disadvantage, especially if opponents force

you to use your weaker foot to kick out from the penalty area.

When kicking from the hand keep your eyes on the ball and throw it well up in front of you. Be careful not to throw it too close to your body because that restricts your movements, or too far away so you have to stretch for it. Keep your head down and follow through with the kicking leg. Your body should be behind the line of the ball to avoid being off-balance and slicing your kick.

Goal kicks

There are three types of goal kick: The simple big boot over the halfway line so that your attackers can challenge for possession.

The short kick to one of your defenders to bring other team-mates into play and start a move.

The chipped kick to loft the ball over opposing attackers to a team-mate in space.

Accuracy is more important than brute force with goal kicking. Keep your eyes on the ball and head down. To gain more height run up at an angle and get your boot under the ball. If you want to get the ball as far downfield as possible run straight at it and kick through.

Throwing the ball out

When you've saved the ball, look up and see if a team-mate is in a good position to start a move. If so, you might decide to throw the ball out rather than kick it. Throwing is the most accurate way of distributing the ball and keeping possession with

The overarm throw and the underhand roll.

Soccer Practice

Using four or five players: stand in your goal facing the strikers who are positioned around the edge of the penalty area 'D'. The strikers take it in turns to shoot at goal. After saving the shot, get back onto your feet as quickly as possible. To improve your speed, the next striker shoots at goal immediately after the previous shot is saved. Vary the exercise by trying chip shots.

In pairs: place a cone to act as a defender at an angle to the goal just inside the penalty-area. Your partner runs up and dummies past the cone and shoots for goal. You come out to narrow the angle and attempt to save the shot. The attacker should vary direction around the cone and shoot with the other foot. Gradually move the cone closer to the goal.

In pairs: stand on the goal line with your back to your partner taking the kick. The kicker shouts 'ready' as contact with the ball is made. Twist to face the shot and save it. Now throw the ball back to the kicker. Repeat the exercise using different types of shot to keep you alert.

In pairs: sit on the ground three or four yards (3m) away from a partner who throws the ball towards you at varying heights and speed. As soon as it leaves your partner's hands, leap and try to save the ball.

In pairs: stand in the middle of a goal, or between two cones placed seven or eight yards (7m) apart. Your partner, 12 yards (11m) away rolls the ball five yards (4.5m) to your left or right. You dive to try to save the ball. After a while, get your partner to roll the ball directly towards you. Race out from your line and dive forwards to smother the ball.

In threes: to practise taking high balls, turning them over the bar or punching them away. The ball is thrown, or crossed into the goalmouth by one player, while another challenges the goalkeeper's attempts to catch the ball.

your team. Roll the ball out underarm if your team-mate is standing fairly close to you. You need to roll the ball into space just in front of him so that he can control it in his stride.

The overarm throw is used to distribute the ball over a greater distance. Use your non-throwing arm to point at the player you are throwing the ball to. This helps your balance. Keep your feet apart, head and body in line with the target and throwing arm straight. Bowl the ball overarm with plenty of power.

Taking steps

Remember the goalkeeper cannot take more than four steps while holding, bouncing, or throwing the ball. Once the ball has been released, it cannot be touched with the keeper's hands until another player has been in contact with it. If this 'four steps Law' is broken, an indirect free kick is awarded and with it the threat of a strike at goal from within the penalty area.

The back-pass rule has been dealt with on pages 16–17.

Dealing with penalty kicks

At a penalty kick the odds are heavily stacked in favour of the penalty taker. The goalkeeper is not expected to make a save. He's a hero if that happens.

Despite the odds, knowing how to deal with spotkicks is becoming more important now that we have penalty shootouts deciding the results of many games.

Remember, the pressure is all on the penalty taker, so try to gain a psychological advantage by looking confident as the player shapes up to take the kick. Attempt to close your mind to all the noise around you and concentrate on the ball. As the penalty taker places the ball try to assess which side of the goal it's going to go.

If a right-footed player uses a straight run-up he's more likely to place the ball to your left. If a left-footed player uses a straight run-up he's likely to place the ball to your right. If the kicker runs at an angle, chances are he's going to bend the ball with pace in the same direction he's running. A blaster will try to hit the ball high into the net.

But whatever method the kicker is using stay on your line and in an upright position for as long as you can. Move your body a little so you are in a position to shift your feet quickly when you have decided in which direction you are going to

Argentina's goalkeeper Luis Islas takes the ball off Nigeria's Rashidi Yakini to break up this attack during the 1994 World Cup.

throw yourself. But don't be too disappointed if you fail to make a save.

Learning the angles

Good positioning is a vital part of a goalkeeper's game and one of the most difficult skills to learn. Shots are easier to save with good positioning. Goals are easily scored if a goalkeeper stands rooted to a spot on the goal line. The aim is for the goalkeeper to appear as a large obstacle to an opponent and ensure that as little of the goal can be seen by the attacker as possible.

To do this the goalkeeper must come off his line and move towards the attacker, narrowing the angle of the target area. Timing is important. Come out too far or too soon and attackers dribble the ball around you; come out too slowly or not far enough and the attacker can come in

close with a large target to aim for.

It's also important to remain on your feet with arms outstretched, presenting as large a barrier as possible to block the attacker's route to goal.

If the attacker runs in from the flank, move across to narrow the angle and position yourself on the near side of the goal so you have the space to stop a cross.

The Wales goalkeeper Neville Southall is brilliant at getting himself in the correct position for any situation. He often makes great saves look easy because he has positioned himself in exactly the right spot to take the ball cleanly. Spectacular goalkeepers are rarely the best goalkeepers.

During corner kicks you should position yourself towards the post furthest away from the ball. You will then have space to be able to move forwards when the ball is kicked.

Tactics

YOUNG players should concentrate on learning the basic soccer skills and simply enjoy playing before trying to understand the different systems and tactics that are now very much part of the modern game.

But as you progress it is essential to have an understanding of the formations and patterns of play. Soccer is a team game and the manager, or coach, should decide on a system that makes the best use of the players available to him. A good playing system uses players' strengths to the full and covers up their weaknesses.

But systems alone do not win games. It is the players working within the team formation who get the results. So, it's important that the manager, or coach, explains the system to all the players in the squad to ensure they are familiar and happy with their roles.

No system, nor tactics, should ignore the individual talents of the team's more skilled players. Everyone likes to see players performing their magic in games, but those skills should be used for the benefit of the whole team.

Basically, tactics are plans from which teams work to get the ball into the opposing danger area to score goals and to stop their opponents from doing the same.

Before the great Hungarians defeated England 6–3 at Wembley in 1953 with a new style of play, the then-prevalent English game was based on 2–3–5 formation: a goalkeeper, two fullbacks, a centre-half, two halfbacks and five forwards (two wingers, two inside-forwards and a centre-forward).

The Hungarians played with a centre-forward deep in midfield and with two attacking inside-forwards. The England centre-half was pulled out of position, while the two fullbacks stayed deep which gave the Hungarian inside-forwards Kocsis and Puskas space in which to cause havoc.

The result shocked world football and within a few years the Hungarian style of play had completely revolutionised the game. Instead of kick-and-rush, or push-and-run, tactics and systems evolved which enabled teams to make better use of their players and to compete and be successful at the highest level.

The Brazilian World Cup-winning team in 1958 used four defenders across the back to deny the opposing wingers space. From this start, teams began to play with four players forward and two in midfield. So the 4–2–4 and then 4–3–3 systems were born.

Throughout the 1960s and 1970s the game became more defensive with fewer attackers and more players in midfield. Tactics were amended and devised accordingly.

England won the World Cup in 1966 without the use of wingers and the rest of football followed England manager Alf Ramsey's plan. In the place of wingers came midfielders who controlled the game. These days World Cups have been won with teams using five players in midfield with just one attacker, as Argentina did in 1986.

In England at club level, Liverpool has on occasions used a sweeper with three defenders at the back, five in midfield and one man at the front as the lone striker. The reason for this defensive formation is simple: flooding the midfield makes it difficult for opponents to mark the midfielders.

Modern systems work successfully because players are more flexible, with midfield players and strikers often being required to move back to help out in defence, while defenders often support the attack with runs down the flanks.

Soccer is an easy game to play, but tactics and systems are becoming more and more sophisticated as managers, or coaches continually work out plans to outwit their opponents.

So a study of team tactics and formations will help to improve your skills and provide a better understanding of the modern game and how it should be played at all levels.

OPPOSITE: Franco Baresi, of A.C. Milan and Italy, is one of the world's top defenders.

1 TEAM FORMATIONS

A TEAM positions its players in any one of the 17 positions shown in Diagram A. The choice of formation depends on the system chosen by the manager, or coach. All systems should be flexible to take into account weather conditions, the opposition, the competition, venue and players.

On hard, icy surfaces smaller players will keep their footing better than taller ones because of the lower centre of gravity; in wet, muddy conditions strength is required; and players not fully fit could struggle on a hot afternoon.

There is no use playing 4–4–2, if the opposition is playing that way, unless you want to cancel each other out. Good coaches do their homework and use tactics to counter opponents. They work out the opposition's strengths and weaknesses before the game. If the opposing winger is their star player the coach will not want to have a young, inexperienced full-back marking him.

If a team is playing in a Cup competition over two-legs, a draw might be good enough. So, the coach may play

Diagram A

1. Goalkeeper
2. Sweeper
3. Right back
4. Right centreback
5. Left centreback
6. Left back
7. Right half/wing back
8. Central defender
9. Left half/wing back
10. Right midfield
11. Centre midfield
12. Left midfield
13. Right winger
14. Right striker
15. Centre striker
16. Left striker
17. Left winger

a defensive formation, especially if the game is away from home. Teams generally prefer to play attacking tactics at home, on familiar ground in front of their own supporters. If one or two star players are injured, the coach may decide to change the tactics slightly to suit the players who are available.

4–2–4

Different nations tend to play different techniques. For example, 30 years ago, most English clubs used a 4–2–4 or 4–3–3 system. The benefit of 4–2–4 (Diagram B) is that you can have six players attacking, or defending. When defending, two midfield players pull back to help the defence. When attacking they can move forwards to support their strikers. You would also be looking for the two fullbacks to break forwards in support. The success of this formation depends on the ability and stamina of the midfielders to continually link with attack and defence. This is a good system to adopt if your team has two fast wingers and the players able to distribute long, accurate passes to the strikers.

4–3–3

This system (Diagram C) gives you strength through the midfield as you have three players in this area. You can also use seven defensive players and six in attack, depending on which team has the ball. When your team is in possession the three midfield players can make late forward

Diagram B

runs, adding more power to the attack. Use this system if your team likes to build attacks with passes.

4–4–2

This defensive formation (Diagram D), is often used when a team has a shortage of strikers, or a surplus of midfielders. It allows you to get eight players behind the ball when defending. When you are attacking there are four players available to support the strikers with the two wide midfield players being used as wingers. Great strain is put on the two strikers, who must be able to hold the ball under pressure until their midfielders can support them.

5–3–2

The sweeper system (Diagram E) is a defensive formation used for absorbing relentless pressure and launching quick counter-attacks. Although primarily defensive, used correctly it can become an effective attacking formation. When the opportunity arises, the two full-backs push forward to support the three midfielders. Many top Continental teams such as Barcelona use this system with slight variations.

4–5–1

An ultra-defensive system (Diagram F) which is very difficult for teams to break down. When attacking, the ball has to be passed accurately and the midfield players have to break forward to support the striker. At international level, France won the European Championship in 1984 under Michel Platini's captaincy, with five in midfield and a lone striker up front.

Diagram C

Diagram D

Diagram E

Diagram F

Diagram A

Goalkeepers

The prime function of the goalkeeper is to stop goals being scored against their team. However, they are more than the last line of defence, they can be the springboards for attack. The keeper should start an attacking movement by throwing the ball to a nearby team-mate. He could also use a long kick upfield to catch the opposition out. Goalkeepers should take command of the penalty area and keep talking to the defence. If the team is under pressure, the goal-keeper can slow the game down to allow the defence to regroup before releasing the ball. But don't get a yellow card for time-wasting.

Because of their position, goal-keepers have a panoramic view of the whole Field Of Play and can spot problems building up for defenders. They can also see attacking opportunities when spaces occur, or when team-mates are left unmarked. The keeper can also act as a sweeper, moving out of the penalty area with the ball to pass to a defender, or midfield player in space.

Remember, the keeper's positional skills are also vital at all corner kicks, dead-ball situations – especially when organising a defensive wall – and when the opposition is attacking.

A goalkeeper must also be ready for the unexpected, such as a rebound, sliced kick, mistimed pass by a defender, or a snap shot from an opposing striker.

Diagram B

Goalkeeper

Corner kick taken from this direction

Defenders

Attackers

Diagram C

Diagram A shows where a goal-keeper should be positioned to narrow the angle and reduce the target area a striker has to aim at.

A goalkeeper is expected to gather all high balls in the goal area. Diagram B shows where the goalie should be positioned for a corner kick taken from the right. If you're playing as the keeper, you should be in the ideal position to cover the shaded area. Your defenders can adjust their positions to counter the danger when the ball is crossed.

For a fierce drive, or cross to the near post, you should be positioned a yard (1m) or so off the goal line (as in Diagram C) from where you can see the danger and follow the flight of the ball more easily. Notice how the defenders have moved to cover the shaded danger zone behind the keeper. One defender has even moved to stand on the goal line.

A goalkeeper is responsible for organising the defence for free kicks around the penalty area. This must be done quickly. In Diagram D, a free kick has been awarded about 25 yards (23m) from goal. The goalkeeper has positioned a wall of four defenders ten yards (9m) from the ball, with defender (A) standing slightly outside a line between the ball and the near post. If the keeper's line of vision is reduced, it may be better to take defender (B) out of the wall. The goalkeeper now has a large area of goal covered and can move forward, or along the goal line to save the ball if it gets past the wall.

Diagram D

Fullbacks, Sweepers and Centrebacks

The fullback's task is to mark, cover and tackle. Essentially, playing this position, you have to stop attacking moves by closing down the opposing winger and force the attack to go inside to prevent the ball being crossed into the goal area.

You should also cover your centreback, protect the goalkeeper, clear the keeper's lines when under pressure, support the midfield and link up with the wingers. Modern fullbacks also attack down the flanks and get crosses in at every opportunity.

Italy's Paolo Maldini has all the necessary qualities to be a top-class fullback, and in the 1994 World Cup showed himself to be the world's best. Two excellent attacking fullbacks are Jorginho and Leonardo, both of Brazil.

You also need to have the pace to match the winger you're marking. If you have no wide player to cover, you should support your defensive partners and look out for opposing players making late runs so that you can block their path to goal.

Sweepers

The 'Sweeper' (Diagram A), or 'Libero' as this role is called in Europe, does not have to mark anyone in particular. When playing this roving role behind the back three or four, you should be ready to intercept attackers who have made late runs past the central defenders. As a sweeper, you should be ready to collect or 'sweep-up' any loose balls. You should also be a good tackler, header of the ball, passer and reader of the game. From the sweeper's position behind the back four you should be able to spot attacking moves building up. The sweeper can also perform a vital attacking role. Generally you are unmarked and know exactly where team-mates are positioned.

The former Bayern Munich and West Germany star, Franz Beckenbauer, was a very successful attacking sweeper during the 1970s. As a former midfield player, 'Der Kaiser' (as he was nicknamed) was able to collect the ball deep in his own half and then set off on a run, or start an attacking move with a long, accurately flighted pass.

Excellent distribution is a vital factor and one of the best examples of the last decade is Holland's Ronald Koeman.

Centrebacks

Most teams have two centrebacks who are the kingpins of defence. In this position you're covering the area where attackers most want to be and so you are under almost as much pressure as the goalkeeper. Any mistake you make could lead to a goal. You must develop a firm understanding with your centreback partner. It is important that each of

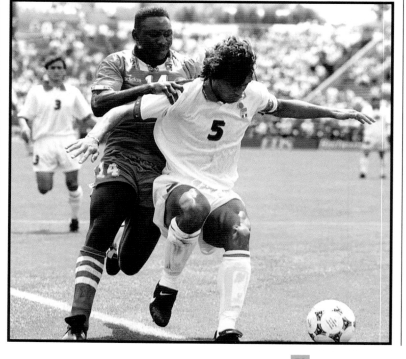

Nigeria's Daniel Amokachi can't get arund Italy's brilliant defender Paolo Maldini during their World Cup '94 match.

Two attackers (reds) are about to put pressure on the centrebacks and work an opening. The left back reduces the threat by moving across and covering his central defenders.

you knows when the other is about to make a challenge, so either can provide support. The taller of the two normally takes the more central position because of the obvious advantage in the air dealing with crosses and defensive headers. The other centreback will play diagonally behind, ready to deal with movements along the ground.

Power in the air is essential for centrebacks. You must completely dominate the strikers you're marking, especially in the penalty area. Often this means giving away a corner, instead of heading the ball out into space where an alert opponent can seize on the clearance and shoot for goal, or maintain the pressure by crossing back in the danger zone. Centrebacks must have the pace to move forwards in attack and to recover if they get caught out of position, or mistime a tackle. If you are the taller player you will often support attacks at corner kicks, where your aerial power can do a great deal of damage. Players in this position often make ideal captains. Franco Baresi of Italy and Bobby Moore of England's 1966 World Cup-winning team are both excellent examples.

Diagram A The sweeper (X) supports his back four. The arrows show potential runs by attackers.

Midfielders

The midfield is where most games are won or lost. Take command of the midfield and you'll dominate the match. So, good midfielders are essential to all teams. They are soccer's Jacks of all trades.

Essentially, they must possess the vision to read a game, have good ball control, pace, the ability to tackle, mark and distribute the ball over short and long distances. Midfielders are the play-makers, the brains, the engine room that drives a team, the vital link between defence and attack. They break up attacks by the opposing team, start attacks for their own side, close in for the kill and even shoot at goal if the opportunity presents itself.

Because midfielders do more running than any other player on the field, they need excellent fitness and stamina. Top class midfielders to watch are players such as Enzo Scifo of Belgium, Italy's Dino Baggio, Balakov of Bulgaria, Demetrio Albertino of Milan and Italy, Germany's Thomas Doll, Holland's Wim Jonk, the U.S.A's John Harkes

Germany's Lothar Matthäus is tackled by Brazil's Dunga. Both these great midfielders are equally comfortable in defence.

and England's Paul Gascoigne.

A strong tackling midfield player can usually operate in a more defensive role by winning the ball and containing the opposition in the central area before driving his team forward – rather like former England and Manchester United captain Bryan Robson.

Skilled ball-playing midfielders are better equipped to break forwards quickly with the ball to start an attack, or hold the ball until a team-mate can move into position.

Midfielders must be prepared to do a great deal of unselfish running with-

Diagram A

The triangle system.

Diagram B

Attackers (A) and (B) are being marked by two defenders. Midfielder (C) runs into space to support (A) and (B).

out the ball to support team-mates in the last two-thirds of the pitch. Clever running off the ball creates space, gives team-mates various options and catches opposing defenders off guard. They might be distracted by your movement long enough to allow a team-mate to dribble past, move into the extra space provided or make a defence-splitting pass.

An attacking midfielder in possession of the ball often has to decide whether to hold on to it allowing team-mates time to move into posi-

tion, or to deliver a short, or long pass. Passing the ball is obviously the quicker of the two options.

Long passes delivered from midfield behind defenders can launch quick attacks, bending the ball with the inside or outside of the foot around them. If you're playing against a team with a sweeper, passes out to the wings are much more effective than dribbling through the packed defence.

Most midfield play operates on the 'triangle' system that allows each

player at least two options of where to pass the ball (see Diagram A).

Supporting the front-runners is an essential part of midfield play. In Diagram B the midfielder runs into space to support the two attackers who are being closely marked by defenders, giving them another option.

A long accurate pass through a crowded midfield area (see Diagram C) can often create a scoring opportunity if players are quick to spot the move and run off the ball.

Diagram C

Midfielder (A) delivers a pass to (B). The defenders are pulled out of position by attackers (C, D, E) and (F) running off the ball.

Strikers and Wingers

Goals win matches – so it's not surprising that top goalscorers are the most wanted and valued men in soccer. Today's ace strikers, like Manchester United's £7 million-man Andy Cole, England star Alan Shearer, Holland's Marco van Basten and Germany's Jürgen Klinsmann, are worth their weight in goals because they have the natural ability to put the ball in the back of the net. They have an insatiable hunger for goals.

As a modern-day striker, like Brazil's brilliant Romario, you need to have pace to lose a marker, strength to hold off challenges, ball control to retain possession and beat an opponent. You must also have the courage to take the knocks that occur when tightly marked, and the confidence to keep shooting even when the going gets tough.

But good forward play by a striker concerns more than just scoring goals. You should be able to set up chances for team-mates, by acting as a target man, or a decoy, to draw defenders away from the middle of the pitch and create space for them to exploit.

In this role, you often receive the ball facing your own goal and should be comfortable when balls are knocked in to you from all areas of the pitch. Be like Welsh international, Mark Hughes. His strength and determination enable him to knock the ball down into the path of a team-mate who is running into the penalty area, or six-yard box to shoot for goal. Sweden's Martin Dahlin is another good example.

As the target man you must make yourself available throughout the whole match, and be prepared to have a constant battle with defenders as you wait for crosses and passes from team-mates.

But whether you have the mobility of Jürgen Klinsmann or the strength of Mark Hughes, you should always be concentrating, trying to anticipate the unexpected and be ready to seize a half-chance in front of goal.

Good strikers do not wait for chances to open up; they are continually on the move looking to play their part in attacking moves. In Diagram A, the striker A has collected the ball on the halfway line, passes to B who passes to C, who crosses for him to score after making a well-timed run.

Wingers

Wingers are usually attacking midfielders who play wide on the flanks. The old-fashioned wingers would wait for the ball to be passed to them. Recent equivalents, such as Marc Overmars of Holland and Russia's Andre Kanchelskis, are expected to attack, defend and go looking for the ball if necessary.

Diagram A

Striker (A) starts and finishes a goal-scoring move. He passes to (B), who passes to (C), who crosses for (A2) to score.

England international Ian Wright in spectacular action during Arsenal's 1993–94 European Cup-winners' Cup tie against Paris St. Germain.

vision to know when to hold the ball up (retain possession) until support arrives, when to cross early and when to cut inside to attack the target. There is no use a winger making a dazzling run down the flank and crossing the ball if there's nobody available. Equally there is no point in running inside to the penalty area if it's crowded with players.

When a fullback makes a break down the flank, the winger should be prepared to drop back and cover that position if possession is lost. Wingers and fullbacks generally work together to create an overlap. This involves a winger in possession passing to an unmarked teammate on the flank. He then runs around his marker to either receive a return pass in stride from the overlapper or act as a decoy, leaving the marker stranded. The problem with the overlap is that if an attacking player loses possession they are both left out of position (Diagram B).

Wingers create space on the flanks, run at fullbacks and cross the ball to their central attackers from the touchline, or move inside to shoot for goal. Crosses made from the goal line must curve away from the goal. If a defender is running back with an attacker he will find it hard to clear the ball without conceding a corner or throw-in near his line, while the goalkeeper may struggle to reach the cross.

Obviously wide players need pace. They must also have the

Diagram B

Defender (A) passes the ball to his winger, (B). Defender (A) then runs around his marker to take a return pass from (B).

Switching the point of attack

Defenders are vulnerable when they are pulled out of position by opponents who suddenly switch the point of attack and get the ball into space where there is no cover.

They are also handicapped when forced to turn by an attacker who gets in behind them. A 'switch movement' by an attacker can often unbalance a defender because he is forced to turn around in order to keep the game in full view. Teams will switch the direction of play by building an attack on one side of the pitch, say the left. So the defence shapes to cover the left side, anticipating a break-through. In doing so, if the defence leaves a gap on the right side, an attacker should run into the space ready to take a pass from the left.

The player with the ball should then switch the point of attack with a pass across the pitch to his team-mate who has just run into the open space. This movement forces the opposing defence to regroup to deal with the new situation, costing them the advantage.

But forwards are not the only players who can switch the direction of play to build an attack. The goalkeeper should be looking to throw the ball out to the wings at every opportunity. A fullback pushing forwards might get in two or three passes on his side of the pitch and then switch play with a 30-yard (27.5m) pass to a team-mate on the opposite flank. Suddenly switching play in this situation also gives the defence a chance to get back into position before losing possession.

This tactic can be particularly effective when making a direct attack on goal. In Diagram A the central striker (A) begins to move towards the right flank where team-mate (C) is running, with defender (X) covering. But (A) suddenly turns and passes to his left winger (B) who is in the space created by defender (Y) moving across to cover central defender (Z) against the

Diagram A

Diagram B

threat developing down the middle.

Switching the direction of attack requires good vision and an awareness of the pattern of play being used by the opposition. Pace, accuracy, anticipation and determination are obviously important. So is feinting to deceive opponents.

Italian defender, Paolo Maldini, is one of the finest examples of a player with the ability to turn defence into attack with a long pass or penetrating run.

In Diagram B, attacker (A) shapes to pass the ball to (A1). Defender (B) moves across to cover, but (A) switches play and passes to (A2).

In Diagram C midfielder (A) has possession and two team-mates (B) and (C) move into position to receive a pass. Midfielder (A) suddenly turns towards team-mate (B) on his right. At the same time a second midfielder (D) runs through the gap created by attacker (C) moving out left and takes a pass from midfielder (A) leaving him with a clear run on goal.

Diagram C

In this example attackers (B) and (C) make decoy runs allowing (D) to make an unchallenged run into the penalty area. An accurate pass from (A) leaves (D) with a good scoring opportunity.

(4) COUNTER-ATTACKING

ATTACKS can start as soon as the ball is won. Counter-attacking begins when the defending team waits for the opposition to attack, then wins the ball in its half of the pitch and gets it forward as quickly as possible.

Attacking teams must always be aware that they can be caught out with a quick counter-attack if they lose possession after getting too many players forward.

Speed is the essential element of successful counter-attacking once the ball has been won. At least one player should be positioned wide to receive a pass and hold the ball to give supporting players the opportunity to make their runs into the opposing penalty area to meet a cross, or return pass.

Diagram A

Defender (A) gains possession, passes to (B) who runs forwards. (A) runs inside and receives the ball from (B) to shoot.

Diagram B

Defender (A) wins the ball in his own half and lofts an accurate 30-yard pass to (B) who is in a good position to run for goal.

Support Play

Good counter-attacking also depends on other members of the team playing a supporting role by pushing up to get opponents out of the half. They should also be ready to pounce on loose balls from hasty clearances or rebounds.

Defenders often make good counter-attacking players after gaining possession. In Diagram A right back (A) has won the ball and quickly passes to his winger (B) and shouts 'Hold it (and the player's name)!' Right back (A) then runs wide and behind his winger. When level with the winger he calls for the ball back and runs towards the opposition penalty area to either shoot for goal, or cross to team-mate (C) who has made a good forward run.

In Diagram B defender (A) has gained possession to break up an attack. He spots striker (B) in an onside position inside the opposition half and delivers a 30-yard (27m) pass to set striker (C) off on a run at goal.

Playing in the 'hole'

This is a term to describe a player who plays, or pushes up into an area just behind the two main strikers (see Diagram C). The player could be a midfielder, a winger or even another striker taking up that supporting position.

Playing in the 'hole' can prove an effective attacking tactic because it gives the opposition's midfield and defence a problem as to who should be marking the extra player.

It is important to inspire in all of your attacking players the confi-

Diagram C
Player (A) moves forwards into the 'hole' behind the two attackers.

dence and ability to take on defenders in one-to-one situations. In modern football, defences are so well organised that it is often the dribbling skills which can make all the difference between success or failure when sides are evenly matched.

THE LONG-BALL GAME

THE long-ball game in many people's eyes has a poor reputation. They claim this direct style of getting the ball forward to the strikers as quickly as possible requires little skill and reduces midfield play.

But it's unfair criticism of what can be a very effective style of attacking play. The long-ball game demands a very high level of skill when used correctly, not only from the passer of the ball but also from the receiving attacker.

When making a long pass make sure the ball lands behind a defender. If the opposition is playing with a sweeper, the ball should be lofted to the wings. Against a tight defence, a long-ball pass down the centre to a team-mate who has made an angled run can often catch the opposition out and result in a goal being scored.

In October 1993, Sampdoria's Roberto Mancini hit a 45-yard (40m) pass to Ruud Gullit. It enabled the Dutch master to strike a thunderous 30-yard (27m) shot past the Milan goalkeeper to give his team a 3–2 victory over the Italian Champions. Nobody considered Sampdoria a boring and unimaginative team!

The long-ball down the middle of the pitch is an excellent way of beating a well-organised offside trap, because the runner comes from deep to chase the ball. Very few defences have the confidence to stick to their tactics when their line is breached by a player running from inside his own half.

Who does what?

There are two elements to the long pass: the passer's accuracy in finding a team-mate at long range, and the skill of the receiver to control the ball and then create, or take the chance that comes from the pass.

In the late 1970s and early-1980s, France's Michel Platini was one of the world's greatest players because of his superb all-round football talent. He was probably the best passer of a ball ever to play for France. But no one remembers quick one-twos with Alain Giresse, Jean Tigana, Didier Six or Dominique Rocheteau; what the fans remember is when Platini sprayed passes all over the field, more often than not finding team-mates in good positions.

Platini's passing skills would have been wasted if he didn't have players around him who could do the

The four diagrams here show the long ball that led to France's goal against England in the first round of the 1982 World Cup in Spain. France, in white shirts and blue shorts, are attacking from right to left. England are in red, white and blue.

An England attack breaks down deep in France's half of the field. The French now launch a counter-strike of devastating simplicity.

Michel Platini intercepts the ball and plays a 10-yard pass to fellow midfielder Alain Giresse. The England team, however, seems to have plenty of cover.

Giresse takes a few steps with the ball and then hits a beautifully weighted, right-foot pass to split the England defence. Danger looms.

Diagram shows simplified positioning for playing in the channels.

The ball lands perfectly in the path of Gérard Soler, who has made a well-timed run. He deftly controls the ball, and guides a shot past Peter Shilton in the England goal.

simple things: trapping the ball, heading, turning past a defender, timing a run. With these skills, France took the football world by storm, and very nearly reached the 1982 World Cup Final.

The long-ball game, if used as a part of your tactical gameplan, can be skilful and prove a very effective surprise weapon – as the diagrams on these two pages show.

Playing the channels

Defenders can set up moves in their own half of the pitch by delivering the ball into an imaginary channel in the opposition's half (see the diagram top right). Strikers can make their moves knowing the ball will be passed into these areas. The channels are wide areas of the pitch, so unless the ball is hit with too much power it will not run through to the goalkeeper. If the ball is played with quality into a channel and does not run out of play, it can put the opposition under a great deal of pressure.

DURING a game, the ball is out of play almost as long as it is in play. Many goals are also scored when the game restarts from set-pieces. Although there is pressure on the dead-ball kicker to put it in the right place, there is even more on the defence to clear the danger.

Teams must plan and practise taking dead-ball kicks so that players become aware of what is expected of them when they are awarded during a game. Coaches should work on different routines to avoid being predictable. They shouldn't just concentrate on the players taking the kicks, either. The players not involved in taking free kicks also have an important job to do, like making decoy runs and moving into various positions to distract and stretch the opposition.

Free kicks, direct or indirect, can occur anywhere on the pitch and require adaptability and imagination if they're to be successful. Set-plays should be kept relatively simple. Involving too many players often results in confusion and a wasted opportunity.

It's best to have two, or at most three players line-up to take a free kick. This keeps the opposition guessing as to which player is going to take the kick, and whether it's going to be a shot, a pass or a floated cross.

Quick free kicks

When you are taking a free kick or corner kick, it's best to cross the ball with plenty of pace. This is far harder to defend against than letting the ball 'hang' in the air, and restricts the possibility of the defence rectifying a lack of concentration in its marking.

Providing the referee lets you, and your players are where the situation calls for them to be, quickly taken free kicks keep the game flowing and don't allow the opposition much time to organise a defence. They also guarantee possession being retained – so often a free kick is squandered unneccessarily.

Throw-ins

A throw-in taken deep in the opposition's half of the pitch can be an effective attacking weapon. It should always be regarded as an opportunity to make a through pass and not merely a means of restarting play. The player taking the throw is often

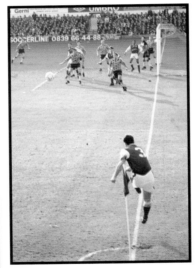

For a right-side corner, ipswich have a left-footed player taking this near-post, inswinging kick against Arsenal.

left unmarked and is therefore in the ideal position to receive the ball back. In this situation, throw the ball to the feet of the receiving team-mate, who can more easily control and return it.

When a team-mate has moved away from a marker, aim to throw the ball alongside the player so that it can be taken on the stride.

Use a long-throw player when the ball goes out of play near the opposition's penalty area. The long reach is an opportunity to get the ball to the opposition goal's near post.

Corners

This excellent attacking opportunity can be played to wherever you feel you have the best chance to take advantage of the situation. Inform your team-mates of the intended target when taking a corner kick. This information can be relayed by previously agreed hand signals (like calls in American football, these should be kept secret). Keep the signals simple, though. One raised arm might mean an inswinger, for instance, two raised arms an outswinger.

Near-post corner

The target is the corner of the goal area and the near post for an

Diagram A – Inswinging corner

attacker to run in and flick the ball on at an angle, or deflect in backwards. This inswinging corner (see Diagram A) is particularly difficult to defend against because it provides the attacking team with options to alter the attack.

Far-post corner

The basic corner kick, aimed at the far side of the penalty area and far post, is easier to defend against than the near-post variation (see Diagram B).

The cross has to be accurate over a longer distance. Defenders have more time to deal with the threat and goalkeepers see more of the ball, making it far easier to attack and collect.

It is important to position players at the near post to block the goalkeeper's view and keep defenders guessing. The kicker should curl the ball into the penalty area for a tall attacker to take the height advantage and head at goal, or knock the ball down to cause confusion, or into a team-mate's path to get a shot in.

The short corner

If the kicker spots an unmarked team-mate close in, there's an option to play a short pass. The receiving player can either take the ball along the goal line before crossing, pull it back outside the penalty area for a

long shot at goal, or play it back to the corner taker who has run wide.

Short corners can force defenders out of the penalty area leaving gaps behind them for the attacking team to exploit.

Attacking free kicks

Any free kick awarded up to 25 yards (23m) from goal is a potential scoring opportunity for the attacking team, as defenders have to be ten yards (9m) from the ball. A free kick within shooting distance also forces the opposition to set up a defensive wall.

You can cause this defensive wall serious problems by bending the ball around it, but it's a move requiring great skill. England defender Stuart Pearce scored from a brilliant curling free kick for Nottingham Forest against Tottenham Hotspur in the 1990–91 FA Cup Final. Another option is to side-foot the ball into the path of a team-mate for him to shoot for goal.

When free kicks are taken, placing attackers in the opposition's

wall can unsight the goalkeeper and upset the defenders – they concentrate on the interloper rather than the kicker. An attacker in the wall can also move just as the kick is taken, making a hole for the kicker to aim at. If the shot goes through the wall, the goalkeeper may not see the ball until the last moment. Also have one or two players making dummy runs into the penalty area to confuse the opposition further.

Penalty kicks

Taking penalty kicks is all about confidence. If you are not happy about taking a penalty, don't! Placing the penalty kick needs great accuracy. Choose the spot you are aiming at and go for it – don't change your mind during the run-up. Aiming at the corner of the back of the net makes it virtually impossible for the goalkeeper to reach the ball. A little sway, or feint of the body as you run up makes it more difficult for the goalkeeper to predict which side you are aiming at.

Blasting a penalty kick relies on power and accuracy. With the longer run-up necessary, more care is needed in deciding where to put the ball. Once the run's started, stick to your decision and keep your eyes on the ball, not the goalkeeper. Get your body over the ball and strike low, following through with the kicking leg.

Diagram B – far-post corner

Near post

⑦ COVERING AND MARKING

ALL SUCCESSFUL TEAMS are built on well-organised, strong defence. The main task of any defence is to stop the opposition scoring by marking attackers closely and denying them the space in which to move with the ball.

Good defending is also about winning the ball back as quickly as possible and launching counter-attacks.

In the past, defence mainly consisted of a goalkeeper, two full-backs who marked two wingers and a big, tall centre-half who controlled the central-area in front of the goal.

In the modern game, defenders have to be as fast, athletic and as skilled as the forwards they are marking. To defend well you must also have good tactical awareness in order to adjust to the various conditions and strategies of the opposition.

Good defending also relies on teamwork and developing an almost telepathic understanding with your fellow defenders. You must know each other's capabilities and shortcomings; you must also be aware of your team-mates' positions during a game.

Communication is another vital requirement. Defenders must talk to each other constantly. Don't be afraid to shout instructions to team-mates, to warn them of challenges, tell them where and when to pass the ball. A good call in the penalty area, for example at a corner, will often prevent two defenders going for the same ball and getting in each other's way.

It is essential that defenders learn and master the art of positioning. Always ensure you are between your opponent and the ball. Restrict their space by jockeying opponents into positions where they can't be a threat, and don't allow them to get close enough so that they can easily turn you.

World-class defenders, such as Italy's Paolo Maldini, don't commit themselves in a challenge for the ball unless they are sure of winning it (or know a team-mate is covering them). If you fail to win the ball in a tackle, your opponent will have your team-mate to contend with and not be given a clear run.

Diagram A

The defenders have pushed back towards their own goal leaving attacker (A) unmarked. He passes to (B) who shoots.

Diagram B

The defenders (X) and (Y) have
moved across to cover and the
defence is much better
balanced to deal with the situation.

Tight marking

Your actions should always be
determined by the position of the
ball. You should either mark your
opponent closely, drop to cover a
team-mate, or pull away from your
opponent to keep your team's
shape and balance. The closer you
are to the ball the more closely you
should mark.

Close support

Except when you have a
specific man-marking
role (when you follow
your opponent everywhere),
you should drop off from your opponent to cover a team-mate who is
now moving in to mark tightly. Take
up a position close enough to support your team-mate, and be ready
to move in and challenge if he is

beaten. You should also move up
and mark your designated attacker
if the ball is passed to them.

Defensive balance

If the ball is at a distance and
there is little opportunity for an
opponent to make a long pass to
the player you are marking, remain
alert and be prepared to support
your central defenders or provide
cover for a fullback. But be aware
of the man you are supposed to be
marking. He may be waiting for you
to move!

In Diagram A the defenders have
pushed back towards their own
goal, leaving an attacker
unmarked and in a good position
to shoot. In Diagram B, however,
the defenders are more aware of
the situation, having covered a

possible run, and they are better
balanced to deal with the attack.

Safety first

If you are challenged close to your
own goal, you shouldn't attempt to
skilfully dribble the ball into safety
or pass while under pressure, you
should clear your lines as quickly
as possible. The best way to do
this is to play it into touch.

The general rule here is 'play the
way you are facing'. It may seem a
negative tactic to kick the ball into
touch, or even give a corner kick
away, but it is better than losing
the ball in the tackle (or by having
your pass intercepted) in the danger zone. Many goals are given
away by defenders trying to be too
clever in their own penalty area and
losing possession.

Man-for-man marking

There are two principle methods of defending: man-for-man and the zonal marking system. The man-for-man system (as shown in Diagram A) is self-explanatory and the most commonly used by teams.

It involves individual defenders marking one attacker instead of space. When the opposition is attacking, defenders should know which players they are responsible for and follow them closely. When an attack starts, the defence should quickly take-up position, marking man-for-man, especially those close to the ball.

This is a slightly risky strategy without a spare player, because as soon as a forward gets past a marker, the defence is outnumbered, generally leaving the attacking team with a clear run to goal. If an attacker gets through, the nearest defender should go for the tackle, leaving other defenders to cover the player he leaves unmarked.

Ensuring adequate cover of an attacker while the player in possession is being tackled is of the utmost importance.

In Diagram B, when attacker (A) is being tackled by defender (X), defenders (Y) and (Z) are covering attackers (B) and (C).

(Y) and (Z) are positioned slightly behind (B) and (C) so they can react to any movement.

As (C) moves to (C1), (Z) also moves to (Z1) and is ready to intercept the ball or tackle (C).

If (A) dribbles past (X), the situation changes.

Three attackers (A), (B) and (C) are faced with only two defenders (Y) and (Z). If neither (Y) or (Z) leave their men to tackle (A), he will have a clear run to goal. But if (Y) leaves (B), then (A) can pass to (B) with little risk of interception.

The Zonal System

Zonal marking is an effective alternative to man-for-man marking and is often used by British League clubs.

In Diagram C defenders are responsible for guarding their area or zone of the pitch and marking any attacker who comes into it. Unlike man-for-man marking, where a defender will follow his opponent anywhere, the zonal system allows a defender to hand over responsibility to a team-mate if an attacker crosses into the next zone.

Zonal marking requires good understanding between defenders, who must not be pulled out of position. They'll leave gaps if they stray too far out of their zone.

For example, a right winger running down the flank with the ball is marked by the left-back. If the winger moves inside and across the pitch he gets picked up by the defender in the next zone. A midfielder will, of course, need to cover the opposing winger.

Flat back four

This means having four defenders in a straight line across the back. Each player should hold position and pick up any attacker who comes into his zone. Because defenders are in a flat line they must be aware of runs from strikers and midfield players into forward areas.

If an attack comes down the right, the back four should move across in a line in that direction. The defend-

Diagram A

The man-for-man marking system provides solid defensive coverage, but is vulnerable if the ball is played into space.

Diagram B

While attacker (A) is being tackled by defender (X), defenders (Y) and (Z) are covering attackers (B) and (C). If (A) dribbles past (X), the situation changes. Either (Y) or (Z) must leave their man to tackle him or he will have a clear run at goal.

ers should be covering each other and remain aware of the lack of protection on the pitch's left side.

If an attack comes through the middle, the back four should move in to a pyramid formation, which forces the attackers to play the ball out wide. Good communication between the back four players is essential for the system to work well. When it is safe to move up, or to catch the opposition offside, the central defender or goalkeeper should give the order.

Those sides adopting a flat back four frequently protect them with at least one defensive central midfield player. If possession of the ball is lost during attack, the job of this player is to make sure the back four are not exposed to dangerous attacks.

Funnel defence

When a team is pressed towards its own goal, defenders should 'funnel' opponents into crowded areas in the centre of the pitch. Fullbacks stand on the touchline side of their opponents, forcing them to go inside where they have a better chance to intercept the ball and cover each other.

Funnel defence's advantages are: that it stops opponents getting crosses in; means central defenders are not pulled out of position; and attackers are caught offside. If the ball is played behind the back four, the goalkeeper can come out and take it. This system only works when midfielders join central defenders at the back.

Diagram C

Zone 4　Zone 3　Zone 2　Zone 1

Man-for-man marking with a sweeper

A variation on the man-for-man marking system, the defence lines up with players marking their respective opponents. A lone player is placed behind the line, with the task of rectifying any mistakes that might occur. This extra man – the sweeper – doesn't mark an attacker but acts as a safety valve to relieve attacking pressure by barring any opponent beating the defence line (see Diagram A).

As soon as the sweeper has the ball the players in the defence line will need to get free of the opponents they've previously been marking. Playing behind the defence, the sweeper has an overall view of the game and is in the ideal position to intercept through-balls, start counter-attacks with a long pass and even move forwards as an extra attacker. From this rearguard position, the sweeper is also best placed to signal for the offside trap to be sprung.

The offside trap

Before the ball is played, the defence moves out in a line at a given signal (see Diagram B). This often catches attackers offside, or forces them to play the ball back towards their own half of the pitch.

Played correctly, the offside trap can prove an effective method of breaking up attacks and keeping the action as far away from your goal as possible.

Playing the offside trap requires good team work, communication and discipline. But teams should not use this tactic too often in a game. It frustrates the opposition and encourages attackers to take on opponents by dribbling straight through, or to beat the trap with quick passing movements. If an attacker breaks through the offside trap successfully with a carefully timed run, there is

often a clear path through to goal. In fact, many goals are scored by attackers beating the offside trap.

Defensive play at set-pieces

Free kicks can be dangerous attacking weapons because they present the opposition with the opportunity of bringing extra players forward to execute carefully planned moves. But they can be defended against.

Defences are often caught out with a variety of pre-planned moves that result in goals. Set-piece situations are a real test of defences and their organisational abilities.

There are a number of basic rules to follow when defending free kicks. They are:
(1) In training decide on which players your team will use to form a defensive wall in matches;

Diagram A

This system relies on man-for-man marking, with a sweeper playing a roving role behind his defence as a safety valve.

Diagram C

**Defenders move up in a
line at a given signal
before the ball is played.**

(2) Concentrate on the situation because many players lose concentration when the ball goes dead;

(3) Get as many players as possible back behind the ball and switch to man-for-man marking, otherwise the defending team could find itself outnumbered;

(4) Don't get distracted by the opposition moving around and calling to team-mates;

(5) Be aware of threatening blind-side runs;

(6) Leave one player free to pounce on rebounds or clearances from the defensive wall.

Defending set-pieces

Building a wall

The 'defensive wall' is built to protect the part of the goal which the goalkeeper might not be able to reach, as well as attackers' passing movements.

Defensive walls are needed when a direct, or indirect free kick has been awarded in a position from which a shot can prove dangerous. Although the goalkeeper usually organises the wall (to provide a good cover from shots while retaining as clear a view as possible of the attackers) the keeper should not have sole responsibility. Another defender standing ten yards (9m) behind the kicker should judge the flight of the ball and direct the wall with the aid of the goalkeeper.

It's better if your defenders con-

**Wimbledon's five-man wall prepares
to face a free kick.**

centrate on marking opposing attackers – or picking up central defenders who have moved forwards – rather than standing in the wall. Midfielders are the best players to have in a wall, with the tallest standing on the outside of the wall to block a swerving shot. The anchor player in second place should also be tall enough to counter the chip shot. This player must also ensure that the wall is not pulled out of position.

The number of players in the wall should be decided by the goalkeeper. As a rule five or six should defend a kick that has been awarded in a central position near the penalty area (two should be enough for a kick taken from an acute angle at the side of the area). If the kick is indirect inside the penalty area six to seven players should form in the wall.

• The wall should be positioned to cover one side of the goal, allowing the goalkeeper a clear view of the ball from the other side.

• Despite what you may have seen, players in the wall should not link arms because this restricts their movement. However, there are two vital parts which should be protected (see picture below).

• If you're in the wall you should be brave and not duck, or twist your body when the kick is taken, no matter how hard the ball has been struck.

• While staying on the right side of the laws, prevent opponents from getting into your wall. An attacker can stand less than ten yards (9m) from the kick and move away from the wall at the critical moment, leaving a gap for the free kick taker to shoot through.

• If, when the kick is taken, the ball is pushed sideways, players in the wall should not be tempted to charge out of position as a unit. The wall should remain firm, while the defend-

er at the end of the wall nearest the ball attacks it.

• If you manage to block the free kick, you should push out as quickly as possible. This is the ideal moment to take the initiative and launch a counter-attack, while the attacking team still has the majority of its players committed to your half. Your full-backs should break quickly from defence, with the midfielders in support to either run with the ball or pass it accurately.

• When defending set-pieces, move quickly upfield once the kick has been cleared to deny attackers space and to catch them offside.

• Defending against free kicks taken from wide positions is much easier because a direct shot on goal is less likely. If the ball is positioned on either wing a cross will probably follow. In this situation a two-man wall should be enough to prevent a clear shot at goal.

Germany's Thomas Hässler (8) has the Belgian wall on red alert in their 1994 World Cup second round game.

Diagram A

This diagram shows the correct positioning for defending a near-post corner.

Defending at corners

The goalkeeper is the key player when defending corner kicks because he can catch the cross. He should stand just inside the far post a yard (1m) off his line and shout to tell his defenders if he is going to attack the ball. In crowded penalty areas, or for inswinging corners, the goalkeeper may prefer standing halfway across his goal.

Marking should be man-for-man, or zone with defenders positioned between their opponents and the ball but slightly in front of it to give them the space to attack the ball. A defender should be placed just inside each post, standing about a yard inside the post. From this position they can cover shots aimed at the corner of the goal and allow their goalkeeper room to attack the ball without blocking the view.

But some goalkeepers, Bruce Grobbelaar for example, like the six-yard box clear of defenders so that they have room to go for the ball.

For balls played towards the far post at corners, defenders should stand just outside the six-yard box, one in line with the far post and the other in line with the edge of the box and others marking either attackers or zones.

Defending at throw-ins

At short throw-ins the player receiving the ball will probably try to play the ball back to the thrower, so close down the receiver and mark the thrower to compromise this option.

Long throw-ins should be treated like corners and defended as such. Mark the space behind and in front of opponents likely to receive the ball and cut down space in the penalty area.

Defenders have two distinct advantages at long throw-ins: more time is taken by the thrower and it is generally clear where the ball will be delivered. Defenders are also given an opportunity to head the ball clear, since it's usually lofted high into the air towards their goal.

Diagram B
Marking throw-ins should be tight, with one player (X) ready to cover the thrower, who often receives back the ball.

Glossary

Advantage: When a referee decides not to award a free kick to a team because a stoppage would mean they would lose the advantage gained.

Anchor-man (Anchor-player): A mid-field player whose main role is to win the ball.

Angle: Applied to the direction in which the ball is travelling. Goalkeepers come off their line to 'narrow the angle'. Attackers will drop off opponents to make a better angle for a team-mate. Defenders cut down the potential scoring area by moving to cover space between the attacker and the goal.

Back four: The four back defenders who form a line of defence in front of goal.

Back-heel: Striking or passing the ball with the back (heel) of the boot.

Ball watching: Watching the ball, or going to it, and not being aware where your opponent is running to or standing.

Bicycle kick: An acrobatic overhead kick (usually a volley) made with one's back to the target.

Blind side: The opposite side of a player to the ball, or an area outside your marker's line of vision.

Block tackle: A tackle made in an upright position, with the side of the foot facing the opponent.

Booking: See Caution

Box: The penalty area.

Caution: When the referee notes a player's name (and number, if any) for a number of offences, either persistent misconduct or ungentlemanly conduct. After administering a caution (or booking as it is commonly known) the referee will show a yellow card.

Centre-back: One or two defenders who guard the centre of defence.

Channels: Areas of play on the pitch into which balls are played.

Chip: A pass made by a stabbing action of the kicking foot under the ball so that it gains height and not distance.

Close down: To deny an opponent space.

Committing a defender: Ensuring that an opposing defender is brought into play by moving towards him.

Corner kick: A kick awarded to the attacking team when the ball goes out of play over the goal line and was last touched by an opponent.

Covering: When the opposition is in possession, taking a position behind your team-mate, or marking a man or zone, in case he is beaten.

Cross: To play the ball from a wide position into a more central position.

Cross over: When two attacking players switch positions, having run past each other to confuse the opposition.

Cushion control: When a player stops the ball so that his body acts as a cushion to take the pace off the ball and allows it to drop to his feet. This can be done with the chest, the inside of the foot, or thigh.

The D: The arc marked outside the penalty area.

Dangerous play: When players raise either feet above waist height in a way that could cause injury to an opponent's head or upper body. The referee will award an indirect free kick for this infringement.

Dead-ball: When the ball is out of play, having crossed either goal line, the touchlines or when play is stopped by the referee for a foul.

Decoy run: When an attacker makes a run to take a defender out of position with the aim of creating space for a team-mate.

Defender: A player whose main role is to prevent the opposition from scoring.

Deflecting: Changing the direction of the ball without stopping it.

Diagonal run: When players run at an angle either from the wing towards goal or from the middle towards the corner.

Dribbling: A player using ball control to take the ball past several opponents.

Dropped ball: When the referee, having stopped the game while the ball was still in play, restarts the game by dropping the ball between two opposing players. Players can touch the ball as soon as it touches the ground.

Dummy: When a player feints to move in one direction and then moves away in another.

Extra time: A spell of extra play, usually 15 minutes each way, to decide a knockout game when the scores are level at the end of the normal 90 minutes play.

Far post: The goalpost furthest from where the ball is crossed.

Feint: See Dummy

Flank: See Wings

Flight: The trajectory of the ball.

Forward: An attacking player mainly concerned with creating and scoring goals. Also known as a striker.

Free kick (Direct): A free kick from which a goal can be scored without another player having touched the ball.

Free kick (Indirect): A free kick from which the ball must be touched by another player before a goal can be scored.

Fullback: A defender operating on either the right or left side of defence.

Goal side: A defensive position where you go so that you are between an attacker and your goal.

Goal area (or six-yard box): The 6yd x 20yd (5.5m x 18.2m) area directly in front of the goal from where goal kicks are taken.

Goal kick: A kick awarded to the defending team when the ball goes over the goal line (but not in the goal) and was last touched by an opponent.

Half-volley: When the ball is kicked just after it has made contact with the ground.

Hold: Retain possession of the ball.

Hustle: To put opponents under pressure when they have the ball.

Instep: The upper surface of the foot or boot by the big toe.

Injury time: Time added on by the referee to the end of each half to compensate for time lost when players were receiving treatment on the pitch, or when play stops. Injury time is decided by the referee.

Jockeying: When a defender retreats between an attacker and the goal forcing him to go in one particular direction while other defenders move in to cover.

Libero: The European name for a Sweeper (see Sweeper).

Man-for-man marking: When players exclusively mark one opponent.

Midfield player: A player who is neither an attacker nor a defender but links with and helps out both.

Narrowing the angle: When a goal-keeper advances towards an attacking player to cut down the amount of goal the attacker has to shoot at.

Near post: The post nearest to where the ball is crossed.

Offside: When an attacker has less than two defenders in front of him and the ball is passed forward to him.

One touch: Passing the ball first time to a team-mate without controlling it first.

One-two: See Wall pass

Overlap: When a player runs ahead and outside of a team-mate in possession to offer space for a pass.

Own goal: When a goal is scored after last being touched by a member of the defending team.

Penalty area (18-yard box): The area in which a goalkeeper can handle the ball. If a defender commits an offence in this area that is punishable by a direct free kick a penalty kick is awarded.

Penalty kick: A direct kick at goal taken 12 yards (11m) from the goal's centre. While it's being taken, all players except the goalkeeper and penalty taker must be outside the penalty area and the D.

Push pass: A pass made with the inside of the foot.

Run with the ball: When a player runs with the ball.

Running off the ball: When a player makes a run to support a team-mate who has the ball.

Sending off: Players sent from the Field Of Play by the referee after committing serious foul play, violent conduct, foul or abusive language, or persistent misconduct after a caution in the same match. To signal that a player is being sent off the referee shows the red card.

Set play: Any pre-planned move to restart play from a free kick, corner kick or throw-in.

Shielding the ball: Placing your body in such a way as to prevent an opponent seeing or playing the ball. This is not the same as Obstruction, however.

Striker: An attacking player whose main role is to score goals.

Supporting player: A player who positions himself to receive a pass from a team-mate in possession.

Sweeper: A defender who plays behind the other defenders, covering them and tidying up any defensive errors. He's also ideally positioned to launch counter-attacks.

Tackle: When a player makes a challenge and dispossess an opposing player or wins the ball himself with legal use of the feet.

Through-ball: A pass through the opposing defence for a team-mate to chase.

Throw-in: Restarting play after the ball has gone over the touchline. The throw has to be taken by a member of the team that did not touch the ball last.

Touchline: The longer boundary line of the Field Of Play.

Turning the opponent: Forcing an opponent to turn by playing the ball past him.

Two touch: Passing the ball to a team-mate after controlling it first.

Vision: A player's ability to see where other players are positioned and to understand the full range of passing options available.

Volley: Striking the ball while it's still in the air.

Wall: A barrier formed by players to block a free kick near their goal.

Wall pass: Also known as the 'one-two'. A quick pass is made to a team-mate who immediately returns the ball to you. This is similar to kicking a ball at a wall and then playing the rebound.

Winger: A player who plays on the far left or right of the attack.

Wings: The areas of the pitch near the touchline.

Index

ITALICS INDICATES PICTURE